# HOMELAND HEROES

# HOMELAND HEROES

*'From Australian disasters...
heroes are born.'*

## MAL WALDEN

Published by Brolga Publishing Pty Ltd
ABN 46 063 962 443

PO Box 452
Torquay Victoria 3228
Australia

email: markzocchi@brolgapublishing.com.au

All rights reserved. No part of this publication may be reproduced, stored in a retrieval system or transmitted in any form or by any means electronic, mechanical, photocopying, recording or otherwise without prior permission from the publisher.

Copyright © 2023 Mal Walden

National Library of Australia
Cataloguing-in-Publication data

Mal Walden, author. ISBN: 9780645815818 (paperback)

A catalogue record for this book is available from the National Library of Australia

Printed in Australia
Cover design and typeset by WorkingType Studio

BE PUBLISHED

Publish through a successful publisher
National Distribution to Australia & New Zealand
International Distribution to the United Kingdom

"**True heroes** are ordinary people doing extraordinary things; not thinking about what is right, but doing what is right without thinking."

# Contents

Pioneers of Pestilence ........................................................................ 1

From Disasters, Heroes Are Born ................................................... 11

Floods — Water Warriors ................................................................ 23

Drought — Angels in the Dust ....................................................... 34

Fires — Front-line Heroes ............................................................... 42

Shipwrecks — High Seas Heroes .................................................... 55

Cyclones and a personal story from Darwin ................................. 72

Bridges, Mining and Unsung Heroes ............................................. 95

Mining Disasters ............................................................................. 103

Quakes, Quivers and Miraculous Escapes .................................... 114

Trains, Planes and a Black Box of Tricks ..................................... 118

War time Heroes ............................................................................. 132

Heroes of the Past .......................................................................... 144

# Pioneers of Pestilence

*Sydney Cove 1788.*

## Sydney Cove 1788

The storm swept in with unprecedented ferocity. Thunderclaps and lightning accompanied by violent gale-force winds. Most of the new settlers had experienced ferocious gales during their long voyage to this new land but invariably they had been alerted by signs on the horizon.

This apocalyptic storm struck without warning signalling the start of a tempestuous relationship with one of the most volatile climates on earth.

> 'The thunder and lightning are astonishingly awful here...5 sheep, 1 Lamb & 2 Pigs, were found dead, lying under a tree, which was split in a violent manner by the lightning... a heavy gloom hangs over the woods'.
> **Journal extract by George Worgan, First Fleet, HMS Sirius, 20 January 1788.**

Not for the first time had early settlers contemplated the biblical prophecies of the Four Horsemen of the Apocalypse. But as they continued their struggle to establish Australia's first penal colony at Sydney Cove none were prepared for a second horseman silently mounting his steed.

## Heroes or Villains?

As dawn broke on this infamous April morning in 1789, a smoky haze from cooking fires and burnt eucalypts gently rose above the newly established penal settlement where it hung like an ominous light shroud.

It was almost 15 months after the arrival of the First Fleet. Eleven British ships — some the size of today's M`anly Ferry — had brought a total of 1,483 new arrivals.

They included 732 convicts, wives and children. 245 marines with some of their families and over 400 crew and staff under the command of Captain Arthur Philip.

After it became apparent that their original landing site at Botany Bay (Kamay), was unfit for settlement they moved to nearby Sydney Cove in Port Jackson on January 26 (Australia Day). And there they stayed.

From an initial scattering of canvas tents, and grimy makeshift shelters and huts — 'some clad in cabbage palm leaves, others in twigs and clay' — Australia's first penal settlement began scratching out its very survival. Further afield rudimentary farming plots and European-style gardens had been established, along with sandstone quarries, sawpits and shingle-cutting camps where convicts were cutting down trees and preparing timber for more permanent building structures.

Alongside these new arrivals also lived an estimated 8,000 or so Gadigal people of the Eora Nation. They had existed for thousands of years sustaining a diverse and rich culture; a lifestyle that would end on that morning in 1789.

It began with the chance discovery of several bodies lying in a secluded rocky cove. Attention had been drawn to the location by a small fire smouldering nearby. Food and water had been provided for the victims who had been left to die by family and friends who then fled from what they would later call the 'devil, devil'. Within days hundreds of native bodies were being discovered in similar rocky inlets and caves from Sydney Cove to the Heads.

> *'It was truly shocking to go around the coves of this harbour, which were formally so much frequented by the natives as shelters for families in bad weather and now to be seen, men, women and children laying dead; deserted by families and friends and left to perish.'*
> **Vice Admiral John Hunter 1788.**

Historians have since described Australia's first smallpox outbreak as one of the greatest disasters in our nation's history with an estimated loss of at least 5,600 lives in the Sydney area alone.

And if their records are correct in the assumption that the continent sustained an indigenous population of 750,000, it's also reasonable to accept that an estimated death toll far exceeded 250,000 lives.

The impact on their social organisations is also reflected by the selective deaths of elders, pregnant women and children under 5.

Those least affected were aged between five and fourteen and of course, British colonists whom it was assumed had been exposed to the disease during their infancy.

While it has been greatly disputed as to whether the virus was smallpox or chickenpox, the greater debate has always been 'how the virus arrived in the first place?'

The question was initially settled to the satisfaction of the early settlers by blaming the French. Explorer Comte de La Perouse had anchored in Botany Bay for six weeks after the British first arrived. At least one of their company died during this period and was buried on the shore of the bay. However, had the French been responsible, then it's argued the outbreak would have started more than a year earlier.

Subsequent theories have also suggested unsuspecting fishermen brought smallpox to Australia's north from the Islands of Indonesia. However, given the fact that infected victims quickly become incapable of even walking, any such outbreak is unlikely to have spread down the desert trade routes to Sydney.

The more likely source has been traced back to first fleet Surgeon John White, who brought with him tubes of 'variolas matter'.

'Variolas matter' was puss taken from a recovering smallpox sufferer and sealed in a glass bottle to isolate and preserve it to vaccinate any children born in the new settlement.

There is however one disturbing theory that continues to circulate to this day. Was the smallpox virus used in a deliberate act of biological warfare?

Those who raise this theory cite the 1763 American siege

of Fort Pitt, outnumbered by Delaware Indians. The British commander refused to abandon the fort instead giving gifts of blankets infected from a smallpox hospital in the hope of spreading the disease and thwarting the siege.

It is argued that the British marines who landed at Port Jackson had insufficient manpower and insufficient equipment for the tasks they confronted.

Like Fort Pitt, the NSW Penal Colony was facing huge difficulties, including the number of indigenous clans opposing the settlers, and a sheer lack of marines capable of defending the settlement.

It's argued that deploying smallpox may have been the last resort to defend the colony. Whatever the cause, if deliberate, then it's believed the appalling devastation probably silenced anyone in authority from ever revealing the truth.

Historians do appear to agree on one point though. Unless some extraordinary new evidence emerges, it may never be known exactly how the first smallpox outbreak came to devastate Indigenous Australia. But then came subsequent outbreaks.

## Second Wave of Smallpox

On the 25th of May 1881, a young child of a prominent Chinese merchant living in George Street, Sydney, was struck down with smallpox. This second contagion quickly spread to the inner suburbs, and the public reacted in panic.

This epidemic continued until February 1882 and during those nine months, there were a known 157 cases, most of whom were treated at a newly built emergency hospital (later to be named Prince Henry Hospital). Forty of these smallpox cases died.

Meanwhile, as the epidemic swept through the community it stoked huge waves of anti-Chinese sentiment. The colonial government even legislated to restrict all movements between China and New South Wales (goldfields).

There is no reason to presume any direct connection between the Chinese and smallpox, but popular prejudice was fanned by fear and the need for a scapegoat, and the Chinese community suffered as a consequence. There were three widely spaced epidemics including 1830/31 and a long-running outbreak in the 1860s.

In 1980, the World Health Assembly declared smallpox had been eradicated through vaccination, and no cases of naturally occurring smallpox have happened since.

But death would also strike indiscriminately from other diseases and epidemics.

In terms of morbidity epidemics in the late 1860s led to more than 8,000 deaths.

## Scarlet Fever 1875–76

As with measles (1860's) victims of Scarlet Fever (1875) were mainly children, and this led to more than 8,000 deaths Australia-wide, with approximately 1,500 deaths in New South Wales alone.

Restrictions on children attending school were introduced, policies on lockdowns and quarantine were put in place, and doctors cancelled surgery hours visiting the ill at their homes.

Both crises passed without a great deal of public hysteria; unlike new epidemics that would follow.

## Russian Influenza

The 1889–1890 pandemic, often referred to as the "Asiatic flu" or "Russian flu", killed about 1 million people out of a world population of about 1.5 billion.

It was the last great pandemic of the 19th century and one of the deadliest in history.

Russian influenza originated in Saint Petersburg before becoming the first truly global pandemic spreading rapidly by way of new rail and steamship networks taking just four months to circumnavigate the world.

The first cases were reported in Australia towards the end of March 1890, with the outbreak reaching epidemic proportions in Victoria for three or four months, claiming 164 lives. However, it struck in waves with recurrences in 1891/92, the northern winter of 1893–1894, and early 1895.

## Typhoid in WA Gold Fields 1891 (2,000 deaths)

Diphtheria, Tetanus, Tuberculosis and sexually transmitted diseases all impacted Australia's most vulnerable First Nation people.

## Bubonic Plague — 1900

The fourth-deadliest disaster to strike Australia was the Bubonic plague or 'black death'.

When the plague virus first reached Australia on 19 January 1900, the response was one of panic and dread, fuelled by the knowledge of the history of the black death and its lethal potential to spread.

There were 12 major outbreaks in Australia between 1900 and 1925. The first contagion is believed to have come from infected rats on ships arriving in Sydney Harbour.

While it finally peaked in the first decade of the 20th century Government archives show a total of 1,906 victims died and while Sydney was hit hardest, the disease also spread to North Queensland with sporadic cases documented in Melbourne, Adelaide and Fremantle.

The plague led to further improvements being made to Sydney's Quarantine Station as the importance of segregating infected patients from the rest of the community was being recognised in time for the next pandemic.

## Flu Pandemic — 1918

The "Spanish flu", as it became known, overtook the enormous casualty toll from World War I. Some believe it may even have contributed to the war ending.

Figures vary according to sources, but history confirms the 1918 Influenza epidemic which struck one-third of the world's population was the 'biggest disaster' on a global scale claiming the lives of at least 50 million — around one-third of the planet's population.

The Spanish flu was named not because it originated there, but because Spain was the first country to report it. Although there is no universal consensus regarding where the virus originated it is widely believed to have been first identified among American military personnel in the spring of 1918.

With no vaccine to protect against it and no antibiotics to treat secondary bacterial infections, a quarantine strategy together with home isolation and mandatory reporting of anyone with the illness were introduced. The use of disinfectants and restrictions on public gatherings were also applied, although unevenly.

While the pandemic started in 1918, the last year of World War 1, it is generally accepted the virus passed through soldiers returning from the Front and then became more virulent in successive waves.

The virus did not reach Australia until 1919, partly because of strict maritime quarantine regulations at the time.

Yet despite these swift measures, cases of Spanish flu began to appear in Australia in early 1919 — and when it struck it showed no mercy.

The first cases were detected in NSW, followed a day later by Victoria. NSW acted immediately closing its borders to Victoria — in defiance of a national agreement — leaving many people stranded on the opposite sides of their state borders.

Victoria was slow to declare an outbreak, such was its overconfidence in quarantine measures. But once it hit, authorities quickly mobilised by setting up 35 temporary hospitals and closing many schools.

The Melbourne Exhibition Buildings became one of the biggest temporary medical centres, treating around 1,500 patients at a time.

Employers staggered workers' hours to reduce contact on public transport. Schools stayed shut after the summer holidays.

But the virus still spread into the suburbs appearing to follow the path of railway lines and further afield on postal routes.

The pandemic swept across the world in three waves tending to affect an area for up to 12 weeks before suddenly disappearing almost as quickly as it had arrived, only to return several months later.

As the number of cases began to ebb, so too did the authority's vigilance. Just as everybody let their guard down, the next wave struck far harder than the first and claimed far more lives. Then as they began to close the temporary hospitals a third, less severe wave struck.

By the end of 1919 (when the Australian population was just over 5 million), about 40% of the population had fallen ill and up to 15,000 mostly young adults had died, including thousands of indigenous Australians. Many believe the final death toll from the Spanish Flu was far higher than reported.

# From Disasters, Heroes Are Born

## Healthcare Heroes

The Commonwealth Serum Laboratories was established in Australia in 1916 to service the health needs of a nation isolated by war.

It was feared the vital supply of medicines from overseas could no longer be guaranteed. Under its first director, William Penfold, between 1918/19, CSL produced three million free vaccines for Australian troops and civilians.

Over the ensuing years, CSL has remained proudly Australian and stayed true to its promise of saving and protecting lives. It has continued to provide all the latest medical advances including insulin, penicillin and vaccines against influenza, polio and other infectious diseases.

## Polio — 1946/1955

Poliomyelitis, or simply polio as it was commonly known, was first reported in Australia in the late nineteenth century. However, it wasn't until 1946 that the epidemic reached its peak in Australia.

It was a highly infectious virus that invaded the nervous system and in the worst cases caused total paralysis in a matter of hours and many cases proved fatal.

There had been far more lethal diseases in the community, but the fear of paralysis and permanent disability were the most terrifying prospects facing families with young children.

While it was also known as 'infantile paralysis', due to the number of children who were stricken with the illness, it was not exclusively a children's disease.

Major epidemics occurred in the 1930s, 40s and 50s; but it was in 1946 when polio reached its peak.

Hospital wards were filled with paralysed victims bandaged into splints with many families forced to build special wooden carts to simply move their immobile children around.

Adding to the fear of this disease was the fact that no one seemed to be sure how they caught it and no one was entirely sure how to treat it.

It was left to manipulation, callipers and an iron lung where only the patient's head would protrude from the contraption designed to forcibly move the chest up and down to enable the patient to breathe. Basically, to remain alive.

**Polio**

In 1955 American Dr Jonas Salk announced that he had successfully trialled a vaccine.

Salk's Australian colleague Dr Bazeley then quickly ensured the vaccine was made available for local use and thousands of school-age children lined up for their injections.

It is estimated that a minimum of 20,000 — 40,000 victims

suffered 'paralytic' polio in Australia between the 1930s and 1960s and up to 1,013 lives were lost.

Actual figures for the number of people 'infected' with the virus are believed to be even greater.

Survivors from the original epidemic are now among our ageing population.

A number of these are still living with a range of symptoms and conditions attributed to what was once one of the most feared disasters to strike Australia. But the fear of pandemics would continue.

## HIV/AIDS from 1983

All the worst aspects and responses to epidemics surfaced in the early 1980s with the appearance of HIV/AIDS.

When first diagnosed in Western society it became known as 'the gay plague' with consequent effects upon both gay communities and individual homosexuals.

At its peak in the early 1990s, about 1,000 Australians died from AIDS each year. Today the number is so low, that it is not even recorded.

## Bird Flu — 1997

Avian influenza — known informally as bird flu — was a variety of the H5N1 influenza strain caused by viruses in birds. More specifically chickens from which infections were directly acquired by humans.

The first case of bird flu in humans was reported in Hong

Kong in 1997 and immediately raised fears that the virus would ignite a human pandemic reminiscent of the catastrophic 1918 Spanish flu.

Emergency plans were drafted and experimental H5N1 vaccines were created. While never reported in Australia the overall human death toll was low — in the hundreds — claiming the lives of six out of ten who contracted the virus.

No one knows precisely how this major threat to human health so suddenly ceased yet we have been warned the situation could change in a heartbeat.

## SARS — 2002

The first outbreak of SARS (Severe Acute Respiratory Syndrome) was reported in China in November 2002.

History is full of ironies. A fatal period of hesitation among Chinese authorities to take immediate action spawned anxiety and panic across the country and indeed among health authorities around the world.

Once the Chinese government launched its crusade against SARS, the outbreak was effectively brought under control and eliminated by mid-August 2003.

But by then it had spread to 30 other countries including Hong Kong, Taiwan, Vietnam, Canada and Singapore.

SARS was the first pandemic with a suspected animal virus link having made the jump to humans from a local live animal market. Possibly bats or masked palm civets.

In terms of mortality, the pandemic killed 774 of the 8,094 people infected; a case-fatality ratio of almost 10 per cent. There was only one case of SARS in Australia, a tourist who was diagnosed while on holiday and was successfully treated before she returned to her home country.

## Swine Flu — 2009

A vicious outbreak of influenza in April 2009 was soon found to have been caused by another new virus which had a mix of origins including pigs — hence the name SWINE FLU.

It's now feared the swine flu pandemic of 2009 may have killed up to 203,000 people worldwide—10 times higher than the first estimates.

Researchers also found a 20-fold increase in respiratory deaths in countries like Mexico, Argentina and Brazil, far higher than the tolls in New Zealand, Australia and most parts of Europe.

Despite the Federal Government stockpiling 8.7 million doses of Tamiflu and Relenza by the end of 2009 more than 37,000 Australians had been diagnosed with swine flu. More than 190 Australians died.

## MERS — 2012

Alarm bells rang again in September 2012 when World Health officials first reported an outbreak of MERS (Middle East Respiratory Syndrome) or Camel Flu as it was also known, in Saudi Arabia.

All victims had lived in or travelled to the Middle East, or had close contact with people who acquired the infection in the Middle East.

By the end of 2019, there had been 2494 cases confirmed with

858 deaths, a mortality rate of roughly 36% with most victims reported in Saudi Arabia.

## Coronavirus — 'COVID 19'

Between 8-18 December 2019, an unsubstantiated rumour began to circulate from Wuhan, China, indicating several people had developed pneumonia-like symptoms from 'a mystery virus'. Then all went quiet.

The world was unaware as many as 41 victims were being treated and the toll was rapidly rising.

Unlike previous influenza strains linked to poultry, pigs and camels, this strain was initially believed to have made the jump to humans by way of bats or the scaly pangolin sold live at a nearby local market.

It wasn't until December 31 that health officials in Wuhan confirmed they were treating dozens of cases and made the decision to close the nearby Huanan Seafood market amid fears it was the source.

As concerns began to grow, Australians sought some reassurance that this virus may just become another flu strain.

2019 and Australia had already experienced one of its worst influenza seasons with more than 310,000 presenting to hospitals and health services nationwide. There were over 900 flu-related deaths.

Throughout January 2020 further reports emerged from China prompting worldwide concern.

On 7 January authorities confirmed the name, of coronavirus, a cousin of SARS (severe acute respiratory syndrome).

On 9 January China announced the first death from the virus.

23 January China's health ministry confirmed human-to-human transmission. China isolated Wuhan after 17 more deaths.

25 January the first Australian case of coronavirus was confirmed in Melbourne. A short time later NSW tested 5 suspects.

While the initial mortality rate of coronavirus (COVID-19) was reported to be less than 2%, W.H.O. experts were now warning this virus had the capability of 'spreading faster than any other virus this century'.

One man who had been aware of the implications from the start was local Chinese doctor Li Wenliang who attempted to issue a public warning but was stifled by autocratic leaders. 34-year-old Li Wenliang then contracted the illness in the same hospital where he was treating patients and died on February 6th 2020.

By then it had become a 'global emergency' and then very soon a global pandemic, the fourth since 1918.

Smallpox, Plague, Scarlet Fever, Tuberculosis and childhood killers such as Whooping Cough and Diphtheria are confined to our past.

While each event left its trail of tragedy, it also helped shape our political and social destiny.

Each crisis has tested relationships between states and raised social tensions within families. They have created heroes in health and hospitals and strengthened our understanding of others in our communities — just as they always have.

Australia's first medicine men were of course indigenous. In fact, at the time of the arrival of James Cook (1760), it has been suggested that traditional healers were better at treating their patients than many of the colonialist doctors.

It wasn't until 18 January 1788 that the first fleet arrived bringing 10 doctors on 11 ships. Over the total period of transportation, up to 350 doctors made the voyage to Australia.

Medically the second fleet was a disaster compared to the first.

Of the 1,017 convicts only 715 arrived alive and of those, 500 were sick and/or dying. Although the second fleet brought with it a portable military hospital, medical services were completely overwhelmed.

John White was the first principal surgeon to arrive on the first fleet. While some cast blame on White for the first outbreak of smallpox there is little argument over his contribution to Australia's initial health care system.

Finding a lack of medical supplies encouraged him to explore alternative healing through native flora and in 1788 began distilling eucalyptus oil as a healing source. He established the first hospital in Sydney and stayed until 1794.

The first doctors to reach our newly established colony were generally ship surgeons, even though many were not always qualified. Some were convicts prepared to serve out their sentences.

**William Redfern** (1774 — 1833) had been sentenced to death for his role in the 'Mutiny on the Nore'; a sentence commuted to life imprisonment.

Having received training as a surgeon's apprentice under his older brother he was sent to NSW where he was granted a conditional pardon and transferred to Norfolk Island as an assistant surgeon.

On 19 June 1803, he received a full pardon before returning to Sydney where he began advocating the use of a new smallpox vaccine.

In addition to his work in hospital wards, Redfern established the first outpatient clinic for men mainly from the convict gangs.

Today, Redfern is widely regarded as the 'Father of Australian Medicine'.

**D'Arcy Wentworth** (1762-1827) came voluntarily to Botany Bay in 1790 on the second fleet ship, the Neptune as the assistant surgeon. He had been accused of highway robbery, and although found not guilty, was advised to leave Britain anyway.

As a medical practitioner, Wentworth was distinguished for the tenderness with which he treated his patients of every degree, and especially that class of unfortunate persons whom the charge of the General Hospital placed so extensively under his care.

From the first colonial days, Australia's health system not only slowly continued to flourish but inspired a path for others to follow and in many cases become world leaders in their field of medical expertise.

**Helen Mayo** — In 1909, she co-founded the 'School for Mothers', where they received advice on infant health and training began for Australia's first maternal nurses.

**Howard Florey** — Pharmacologist and pathologist shared the Nobel Prize in Medicine in 1945 for his role in the making of penicillin.

**Frank Macfarlane** Burnet — Australian virologist and 1960 Nobel Prize winner for his contribution to immunology.

**Professor Donald** Metcalf — 50 years of work in Cancer and stem-cell research.

**Edward Dunlop** — An Australian surgeon who was renowned for his leadership while being held prisoner by the Japanese during World War 2.

**Fred Hollows** — An ophthalmologist who became known for his work in restoring eyesight for countless people in Australia and around the world.

**Peter C. Doherty** — Nobel Prize researcher into the immune system.

**Gustav Nossal** — Research biologist famous for his contributions to the fields of antibody and immunological tolerance.

**Fiona Stanley** — Research into child and maternal health, and birth disorders such as cerebral palsy.

**Fiona Wood** — Plastic surgeon well known for her patented invention of spray-on skin which saved many lives following the Bali bomb blasts.

**Ian Frazer** — Researcher who developed and patented the basic technology behind the HPV vaccine against cervical cancer.

**Graeme Clark** — A key figure in the research and development of the Bionic Ear — a multiple-channel cochlear implant.

**Victor Chang** — cardiac surgeon and a pioneer of modern heart transplantation.

Aspro was developed between 1915 and 1917 by Melbourne chemist George Nicholas and his brother Alfred as a form of Aspirin in a tablet.

The 1918 Spanish Flu led to the establishment of the

Commonwealth Serum Laboratories which helped pioneer Australia's vaccine development.

CSL produced three million free experimental vaccines at that time for Australian troops and civilians.

Lithium, discovered in 1948 by Dr. John Cade, became the world-first treatment for bipolar and similar mental health disorders.

Relenza was the world's first anti-flu drug and was developed at several institutions in Victoria and released onto the market in 1996.

Australia not only leads the world in many medical firsts it also helped dispel misconceptions during epidemics that fostered prejudice and persecution against migrant groups within the community.

The 1870s scarlet fever epidemic uncovered much about the living conditions of the city's poor, just as the AIDS epidemic would help heal long-hidden misconceptions about the gay community.

The list of Australian medical firsts is as endless as the tributes reserved for the unsung heroes of health care; the many community volunteers who emerge throughout every crisis, risking their own lives in pandemics to save others.

Louis Pasteur, the man who warned that 'microbes will get us in the end' also offered some positive advice.

*"In the field of observation, chance only favours the prepared mind."*

*Thanks to Jeffrey H. Toney and Stephanie Ishak. The University of Newcastle. Krystal Ha, The University of Melbourne. Historian Christopher Warren.*

National Museum of Australia. Australian National University. Royal Australian Historical Society.

# Floods — Water Warriors

By sheer stealth, the silent black swirling mass rose from the depths, surrounding the township and all within. Suddenly, under a full moon, the silence was broken by piercing screams; each scream preceding the sound of 'crash after crash' as one by one, houses would fall and were swept away with their occupants.

Then, amid this apocalyptic scene came two unexpected heroes.

## Gundagai — 1852

It was in the middle of the night on 24 June 1852, when Australia's most catastrophic flood swept through the New South Wales town of Gundagai. Nearly a third of the population was killed in what remains one of Australia's greatest natural disasters.

In previous floods, residents of Gundagai had sought shelter in their attics and on rooftops, but by the very nature of this flood, there was no escape.

Entire buildings were swept away leaving survivors clinging to treetops where some clung for up to two nights before losing their grip and disappearing beneath the swirling mass. Others died from sheer exhaustion in the branches. The water rose so rapidly and so unexpectedly that it left the population of 250 desperately unprepared.

As the Sydney Morning Herald's Gundagai correspondent wrote after he too was rescued from a tree branch:

'As night drew in, the unavailing cries for assistance all around became fearfully harassing. Crash after crash announced the fall of a house and the screams that followed the engulfing of those who clung'.

When the water finally receded and bodies recovered, only three buildings were left standing. The death toll was estimated between 80 and 100 people, representing over one-third of Gundagai's population. Many believe the toll was far greater, as an undetermined number of visitors were in town when the flood struck.

However, a third of the township was rescued — plucked from surviving rooftops and trees and ferried through the raging current to safety by two Wiradjuri men, Yarri and Jacky Jacky.

For more than 24 hours they bravely and systematically searched for those victims unable to help themselves. They began by launching their canoe upstream before navigating down among the trees in the swirling floodwaters, deftly avoiding fast-flowing logs and debris in their search for survivors.

Their canoe was only able to carry one passenger, so Yarri

made many trips, taking people one at a time. He rescued 49 white settlers while Jacky Jacky saved the lives of another 20 using a recently repaired rowboat.

After each rescue, they trudged back upstream carrying their craft to begin a new sweep down through the treacherous floods.

Despite the conception of frail and flimsy watercraft, the heroes of Gundagai proved most adept in navigating the swirling treacherous waters. What was even more heroic and altruistic, was the nature of saving the lives of those whose racist attitudes towards their people and the dispossession of their land never appeared to enter their minds.

History confirms the skill of Wiradjuri men and Aboriginal freshwater people whose use of bark canoes and ability to make a relatively quick and functional vessel assisted many European settlers in inland regions where no watercraft were available.

When Yarri and Jacky Jacky launched their flimsy canoe into those raging floods of Gundagai they unknowingly began a tradition of rescues and evacuations involving watercraft of every description, time after time and flood after flood.

On the 165th anniversary of the Gundagai floods, a sculpture was finally unveiled in the rebuilt town to honour those indigenous heroes whose deeds far exceeded those of a dog which sits on a tuckerbox just five miles from Gundagai.

* * * *

From official records, which extend further in time than any other Australian disaster, floods account for more than 2,400 lives lost since the first reported flood death in 1790.

To put that into perspective, more than 900 lives have been lost in bushfires.

(NSW Aboriginal Land Council, Bureau Statistics — Australian Yearbook)

## History of Australian floods

### Ipswich, QLD — 1893

The Queensland flood of February 1893 is often referred to as the Black February Flood. There were three floods that month resulting in 35 deaths and more than 300 injured.

The first flood on 6 February was due to a deluge associated with a tropical cyclone called "Buninyong". Both the Victoria Bridge and the Indooroopilly railway bridge collapsed in this deluge.

A second cyclone struck on 11 February, causing relatively minor flooding compared to the first flood but when a third cyclone came on 19 February, it was almost as devastating as the first and left up to one-third of Brisbane's residents homeless.

### Clermont and Peak Downs, QLD — 1916

A cyclone swept the Queensland coast along the Whitsunday Passage, bringing heavy rainfall to Clermont, Sapphire and Peak Downs. This usually flood-savvy town forgot to counter for the runoff from nearby catchments and creeks. The debris it carried with it arrived at crushing speed. The torrent smashed through houses and caused widespread damage. 65 people died, 10 homes were destroyed, 50 buildings were damaged and 10,000 livestock were killed.

The lower part of Clermont was submerged and like the town

of Gundagai in 1852 residents were forced to rebuild the town on higher ground.

## Brisbane, Cairns, Townsville — 1927

A tropical cyclone hit north of Cairns, causing major rainfall through Queensland, reaching as far as Toowoomba. The torrential rain, which fell from 9-17 February, led to the deaths of 47 people, and damaged roads, railways, bridges, and buildings — destroying 16 houses. As with all major floods, there was also widespread loss of livestock. The estimated costs reported at the time were in the region of £300,000.

## Northern Tasmania — 1929

The area of northern Tasmania had always been prone to heavy rainfall over short periods but in 1929 up to 500 mm of rain fell over three days. The floodwater carved a swathe of destruction across the entire region, destroying everything in its path, including vehicles, buildings and railroad tracks.

22 people died, 1,000 homes were damaged and 25 bridges were destroyed. The massive floods also inflicted huge stock losses impacting the state and national economies.

## Melbourne — 1934

When measured in terms of peak water flows, the great Yarra River flood of July 1891 was regarded as the largest since the beginning of European settlement. However, the massive flood in 1934 was not quite as large but as Melbourne had expanded the damage was exponentially greater.

In late November 1934, ferocious storms swept across the city dumping 140 mm of rain in 48 hours. Heavy rain had also fallen through central Victoria and the catchment areas in the hills east of Melbourne. The combined force of floodwaters swept down the Yarra River with catastrophic consequences.

The suburb of South Yarra was first to sink under the swirling muddy water before spreading through the low-lying suburbs of Collingwood, Richmond and South Melbourne.

36 people died including 18 killed by collapsing buildings, landslides and falling trees. More than 400 buildings were damaged in Melbourne and 6,000 people were left homeless.

It was neither the first nor last time Melbourne faced extreme flooding. The city had already suffered in 1863 and again in 1891 but the 1934 flood caused the greatest loss of life.

However, despite its history of flooding and subsequent protective systems that had been put in place, it was almost inconceivable that another flood would strike; a flash flood in 1972, which created some of the most spectacular scenes right through the heart of the city.

## Macleay Valley, NSW — 1949

In late August 1949, the McLeay River in North Eastern NSW broke its banks causing major flooding in Kempsey and low-lying areas of the floodplain. The flood killed six people, destroyed 15,000 livestock washed away 53 homes flooded many shops and destroyed nearly all their stock.

About 2,000 people were left homeless in the deluge described as the worst flood in the history of that area.

## Hunter Valley, NSW — 1955

In February 1955, Maitland and the Hunter Valley experienced what was considered Australia's 'worst-ever flood'. The Maitland flood as it was called was also Australia's first natural disaster to be broadcast to an international audience.

The devastating floods which peaked at 12.5 metres claimed a total of 25 lives, leaving 7,000 buildings and homes damaged and over 40,000 people forced to evacuate.

These floods in the Hunter Valley have become symbolic in the Australian psyche of the dramatic nature of flood damage and promoted the need to establish new rescue procedures. Five of the lives lost were due to electrocution during rescue operations.

## Brisbane — 1974

After a particularly wet year in 1973, Brisbane was inundated with water when tropical cyclone Wanda hit the north of the city on 25 January 1974.

By January 29 the Brisbane area had recorded 900 mm of rain, with 314 mm falling in 24 hours. In the coming months, more torrential rain swept down the east coast, causing further floods in NSW and as far south as Tasmania.

The floods killed 14 people and left 300 seriously injured mainly in the Brisbane area. 56 homes were destroyed while a further 6,000 were damaged at an estimated cost of $68 million.

## Hawkesbury and Georges River Flood, NSW — 1986

On what was dubbed Sydney's wettest day ever, record rainfall reaching 327.6 mm fell in just 24 hours. The torrential rain created chaos, flooding roads and forcing many motorists to abandon their cars. Transport was severely disrupted in the city and trains were halted due to flooded tunnels.

In all 6, people died, and 10,000 homes were damaged, leaving an estimated damage bill of $35 million.

## Brisbane and SE QLD — 2010

One of the most devastating recent floods hit the Queensland capital of Brisbane in December 2010. Thirty-five people were killed, over two hundred thousand people were evacuated, and damage to the economy was estimated at over $2.38 billion.

It was not just one flood, but a series of floods caused by bad weather in the preceding months. Heavy rainfall which began in September 2010 culminated in a final blow when Cyclone Tasha, struck with further rain described as in 'biblical proportions'.

The flooding continued into January 2011, when the Brisbane River burst its banks devastating the capital and surrounding suburbs.

## Catastrophic Floods, NSW — 2022

March 2, the New South Wales Premier Dominic Perrottet described record-breaking rain as a "one-in-1,000-year event".

The mayor of Ballina Shire council in northern NSW warned

residents to expect a 'one-in-a-500-year flood'. Brisbane then suffered what was described as its third 'once in a century flood' in less than 50 years.

Scientists then warned against the use of sensational terminology fearing it risked misleading the public about the likelihood of disasters of this magnitude being repeated. History proved the scientists were right.

It began in the last week of February after a devastating deluge described as an unpredictable 'Rain Bomb' broke all previous records, swamping SE Queensland and dumping one year's rainfall in two days.

The flood-mitigating Wivenhoe Dam was once again forced to release high levels of water eclipsing the devastating crisis of 1974. From Maryborough and Gympie in Queensland, it quickly and unexpectedly swept down the coast, causing 15 thousand evacuations in Brisbane alone. The rain then continued into northern NSW feeding the river systems and isolating dozens of towns causing tens of thousands more evacuations. From Ballina to flood-prone Lismore the water exceeded all previous levels.

By the beginning of March 2022, the entire eastern coast of Australia was completely saturated, from SE Queensland down to the Victorian border. In the first ten days, tens of thousands of homes and businesses were damaged or destroyed in what the Climate Council described as 'one of the most extreme disasters in Australia's history'. 22 people were known to have died, 13 in Queensland and 9 in New South Wales, with flood-prone Lismore, NSW experiencing the worst disaster in its history.

What made this flood different from others? According to the experts, La Nina, climate change and all the elements, combined to create another record-breaking disaster.

Thursday 13 October 2022, just six months after a devastating flood claimed the lives of 20 people down the east coast of Australia, another flood emergency struck.

This deluge triggered mass evacuations in Victoria, New South Wales and the island state of Tasmania.

Melbourne suburbs bore the initial brunt of the storm with flash flooding leaving hundreds of homes underwater.

Over the next three days, thousands more were displaced in central and northern Victoria with as many as 34,000 homes affected.

In a country prone to big swings in weather, scientists conceded this deluge was unusual because it had fallen across almost the entire continent.

From those 'First Nation heroes' who paddled their bark canoes through raging floodwaters risking their own lives to rescue victims of the Gundagai floods in 1852, a similar spirit emerged around the nation.

Described as a massive 'Dingy Dunkirk' some of the biggest volunteer evacuations in Australia's history responded as flotillas of tinnies, canoes, boats, inflatables even water skis came to the rescue of flood victims.

The ADF, which has a long history of helping out when disaster strikes, dispatched thousands of troops into flood efforts.

Once again the true heroes emerged as community volunteers were the first to respond.

The 'Mud Army' was another community-based movement first formed in the wake of the 2011 Brisbane floods. A group of volunteers was initially accused of behaving a little chaotically roaming streets covered in mud. 'Scraping, cleaning and spraying under a false pretence of portraying some mythical qualities of Queenslanders in a crisis'.

Although the actions of the Mud Army violated many of

the accepted rules of disaster response and risk management, according to Lord Mayor Newman their anarchy was worth it. 'Those volunteers saved us millions, absolute millions'.

A statue in honour of the Mud Army heroes has since been erected in Brisbane.

If 'heroes are born out of disasters' then no greater tribute can be found than honouring the spirit of the thousands of community volunteers who are always first to respond, whatever or wherever the crisis.

La Nina has brought wetter summers, especially in the north, and global warming is now being blamed for turbocharging these events. The tragic reality is not so much the subsequent loss of life and the economic impact they inflict on the national economy, but the knowledge that even worse is to come.

Attribution: National Geographic Australia and The Bureau of Statistics.

# Drought — Angels in the Dust

The truck pulled into the Queensland farm raising a cloud of dust as it manoeuvred into a loading bay by the stockyard. An anxious farmer watched as the driver stepped down from his cabin to inspect the forced sale of his starving cattle. It took less than three minutes before the farmer was informed his cattle were in too poor a condition for any market value. The truck immediately left in another cloud of dust.

The distraught farmer loaded his gun, shot all his cattle, shot his working dog and then he shot himself.

From this singular tragedy, two women neighbours launched a grassroots organisation 'Drought Angels' in a bid to help more than 5,000 farming families facing a similar crisis.

## The tragedy of drought

Australia is a continent defined by extremes; droughts, floods, heatwaves, and fires. But, of all our natural disasters, scientists warn that 'heat' is the number one killer.

Today we are forced to add another element that is influencing the forces of nature. A term we call 'climate change', has found us in unchartered waters; either too much water or too little. This we are told is the new norm.

Captains' logbooks from ships anchored off Sydney Cove described the Settlement Drought (1790-1793), was one that 'threatened the very survival of the first settlers in Australia'.

Farmer's records continued to track the impact of 27 drought years between 1788 and 1860 and disturbing accounts of product and stock losses.

Since 1 January 1908, nearly 120 years after William Dawes built his famous observatory at Sydney Cove, the first national weather agency — the Bureau of Meteorology has recorded at least one 'severe' drought every 18 years claiming thousands of lives.

Today science has provided a deeper snapshot of climate extremes with carbon-dated records from tree rings, ice cores, corals, and sediment formed almost one thousand years before our written records began.

From all this information we have determined seasonal rainfall in parts of Northern Australia is wetter than ever before, while other parts of the country are 'unprecedently' dryer. Of this, there is no argument, including official temperatures which have also hit an all-time high.

## Federation Drought — 1901

Searing temperatures that accompanied the Federation Drought from 1895 still hold the record as Australia's deadliest heatwave, closely followed by 2009, which recorded at least 432 heat-related deaths.

And in terms of stock losses the Federation Drought which began in 1895 is still regarded as Australia's 'most destructive drought'.

In 1892 Australia had 106 million sheep, but by 1903 the national flock had almost halved to 54 million. The nation lost more than 40 per cent of its cattle over the same period, nearly three million in Queensland alone.

The drought also ended an established squatter-dominated pastoral way of life in NSW and Queensland with bank foreclosures and the partitioning of large settlements and cattle stations.

Vital river systems across the nation suffered greatly; most notably the Darling River which virtually ran dry from Bourke, New South Wales. The wheat crop was "all but lost", and the drought even threatened Sydney's water supply.

The drought eventually broke in mid-December 1902 when heavy rain spread after first falling across Victoria.

## The World War 2 Drought — 1937-1947

In the second half of the 1920s, the Australian economy was suffering from crippling wheat and wool prices, and competition from other commodity-producing countries. Then came the Wall Street crash of 1929 plunging the world into economic depression. It took Australia almost a decade to recover then came World War

2 and another devastating drought which prevailed predominantly over eastern Australia reaching serious levels in 1937.

In 1938 there was further deterioration in New South Wales and Victoria as it also spread to eastern South Australia and on through the southwest grain-growing region of Western Australia where wheat yields plummeted to their lowest level since 1914.

In Victoria, the drought conditions provided all the elements for the disastrous Black Friday bushfires in January 1939.

While heavy rain fell in late February, dry weather returned again and by 1940 — one of the driest years of the century — southern parts of the country were in crisis. Dams were empty in New South Wales and Brisbane imposed strict water restrictions.

By 1943 the drought had wiped out significant parts of the surviving national wheat crop. Large rivers in NSW such as the Hunter were virtually dry. By April 1945 most Victorian water storage facilities were empty, the Murray River ceased flowing at Echuca and Adelaide too faced water shortages.

The end of the drought coincided with the 1946/47 Ashes cricket series when it rained on all 25 matches, including two tropical rainstorms during the First Test in Brisbane and another in the Second Test at Sydney.

## 1960s Drought

From 1965 to 68, eastern Australia was again greatly affected by drought. Conditions had been drying over the centre of the continent since 1957 but spread elsewhere during the summer of 1964/1965. This drought contributed to the devastating 1967 fires in Tasmania in which 62 people died in one day and 1,400 homes were lost.

## 1980s Drought

The drought in 1982/83 was regarded as the worst of the twentieth century for short-term rainfall deficiencies.

There were severe dust storms in north-western Victoria and severe bushfires in South Australia and Victoria (Ash Wednesday) killing up to 75 people. In Victoria, 47 people died. There were 28 deaths in South Australia.

This El Niño-related drought ended in March when a monsoon depression became an extratropical low and swept across Australia's interior and onto the southeast in mid-to-late March.

## 1990s Drought

This very severe drought began forming in the second half of 1991 before it intensified in 1994 and 1995 to become the 'worst on record in Queensland', affecting a region stretching in a 200 km to 300 km wide strip from Stanthorpe to Charters Towers destroying most of the state's wheat and barley crops. By June 1994, more than ten towns had lost irrigation systems compounded by some areas having received no significant rainfall for five years. A part of the upper Darling River system collapsed leaving more than 13,000 properties struggling to survive.

## 2000 — 'Millennium' Drought

The Australian drought from the year 2000, also known as the Millennium drought, was said by some to be the 'worst since the Federation drought'.

It commenced late in 1996 with low rainfall conditions in south-eastern Australia, particularly during the cooler months from April to October.

The most acute period of the so-called 'Millennium drought' fell between 2001 and 2009 as the great brown stain spread across most of Southern Australia impacting its largest cities and largest agricultural region, the Murray–Darling Basin.

That drought finally ended with the arrival of wet La Nina conditions during 2010 and 2011, with particularly heavy summer rainfall.

## 2020 — Climate Drought

As we entered this new decade, climate experts issued another grim warning:

'Australia's temperatures had peaked at record highs. National rainfall figures had fallen to the lowest on record. 'Two-thirds of Queensland was officially in drought'.

While the debate was raging over man's contribution to global warming a 'rolling furnace' was surging across the nation toppling records and scorching the earth with searing temperatures in the high 40s.

The agricultural sector warned the national sheep flock was expected to collapse to its smallest size since 1904.

Scientists would not specifically blame climate change as the cause of droughts, but definitively claimed 'climate change had made the effects of droughts stronger and more damaging'.

'Extremes, they warned, 'will become the norm'.

## Out of Droughts Heroes are Born

In early 2014 an apparition of angels appeared to rise out of the Queensland dust bowl. Natasha Johnston and Nicki Blackwell had packed a ute with supplies to help their stricken neighbour struggling to cope and was being forced to sell his starving cattle.

When the truck arrived to pick them up, they found the animals too poor for any market value. The distraught farmer loaded his gun, shot all his cattle, shot his working dog and then he shot himself. It was not an isolated case.

So, moved by this growing tragedy the women launched a grassroots organisation 'Drought Angels' in a bid to help more than 5,000 farming families in crisis.

By 2022 through direct personal contact, they had provided financial assistance, food hampers, care packs and personalised support for thousands of struggling farming families across Australia. Within the first 12 months, the movement exploded signing up 41,000 members seeking drought advice and support. Since its inception in January 2014, 'Drought Angels' has expanded its team to assist thousands in need, whether through mice plagues, coronavirus, bushfires or floods.

These elements are an enduring, recurring feature of the Australian landscape which impacts heavily on our social, economic and environmental systems.

While science projects droughts and flooding rains are set to break more records, the survival of thousands of struggling farming families may well rest in the hands of heroes such as the 'Drought Angels' and the Aussie spirit of similar-minded community leaders.

Dorothea Mackellar, 'My Country', 1908

*The core of my heart, my country!*
*Her pitiless blue sky,*
*When sick at heart, around us,*
*We see the cattle die —*
*But then the grey clouds gather,*
*And we can bless again*
*The drumming of the army,*
*The steady, soaking rain.*

# Fires — Front-line Heroes

*Noojee Railway Bridge, 1939 — National Library of Australia*

"... The sky was on fire... the roaring wind driving the flames... with a sound of many locomotives... and balls of crackling fire ... it consumed all it touched..."

Black Friday survivors.

For millions of years, fire has shaped the landscape of the Australian continent.

Many were started by lightning and for thousands of years, Indigenous Australians used fire for hunting purposes and to encourage the regeneration of vegetation.

From days of settlement, the history of Australian Bushfires has burnt an indelible image into the nation's psyche. They not only reflect a tragic legacy but also reveal miraculous escapes and acts of unbridled bravery.

These records also reveal a single haunting memory from survivors — 'it was the terrifying sound' they remembered most.

1939 Black Friday — "Like a great tornado, it sizzled like lightning... blown by a wind of great force... with a sound of many locomotives... it roared as it travelled... balls of crackling fire ... consuming all that it touched".

The first written accounts of bushfires provided just the barest details. They represented the basis of a public news service but were invariably read in the press well after the fires were extinguished.

It wasn't until Black Friday, 1939 when visiting world-renowned science fiction writer and futurist H.G. Wells helped set new parameters with his first-hand descriptive account from the very frontline of Australia's worst bushfires.

## Black Friday 1939

In the early days of January 1939, hundreds of fires had been burning spasmodically across a large part of Victoria although many Australians had been distracted by other events at that time. Not the least being the Spanish Civil War and the impending war in Europe.

Visiting British author and social commentator H.G. Wells had created a controversial storm by describing German leader Adolph Hitler as a 'certifiable lunatic'. He was strongly rebuked by Australian PM Joseph Lyons for using inappropriate language to describe a foreign head of state.

Attending a Scientific Assembly in Canberra, H.G. Wells then published an article drawing a strong analogy between fighting fires and the same spirit required to meet the aggression that was now threatening the world.

Friday 13 January 1939. Melbourne dawned just as the weather bureau had warned. The sun rose fiercely reaching 98.5 degrees (F) by 9 am before reaching 109.6 (F) at midday. Bushfires, which had been temporarily lulled in the preceding days around the state, suddenly sprang back into life with awesome ferocity. Many districts were plunged into a pall of complete darkness as clouds of thick smoke blanketed the sun. And amid the darkness, the fires roared.

On hearing of Victoria's plight, H.G. Wells decided 'there was nothing for it but to go up-wind to the bases of that streaming smoke curtain and see the actual burning oneself'.

Among his first dispatches, he wrote of the 'aggressive' bravery of Australian firefighters as they stood undaunted against the overwhelming and unpredictable fire.

'It advances by rushes, by little venomous tongues of fire in the grass'.

'Its front is miles deep. It is here, it is there, like a swarm of venomous wasps'.

He continually drew lessons from the fires with words that developed into a polemic about how Australia had to defend itself from military attack in the same way it was defending itself from fire: through aggressive prevention.

"There is something exhilarating and quickening about fire, and something right and true about the military metaphors". 'A bushfire is not an orderly invader, but a guerrilla'.

As the world teetered on the brink of WW2, Australia was facing the worst natural disaster in its history and H.G. Wells was at the front lines to hear first-hand from survivors.

'Great clouds of flame leapt from hill to hill, driven by windstorms that carried masses of inflammable gas. Dull booming sounds were heard in advance of the walls of flame. Solid metal melted in the heat'.

The fires were accompanied by record temperatures and winds that reached velocities estimated at over one hundred miles an hour. But it was the sound most remembered.

'We could hear the fire coming ... like a great tornado it sizzled down like lightning; you could see it, and nothing on earth would have stopped it'.

Around the Victorian town of Matlock, the force of the fire sucked trees from the ground and threw them across the landscape, 'as though a giant had strewn a box of matches'.

When rescuers finally reached Fitzpatrick's Mill they found a lone survivor from 15 men who had perished.

George Sellers said he would live with the sounds of that firestorm, including 'the screams of the men and the horses' to the end of his days.

When it was all over, large areas of the State presented scenes of absolute desolation.

Journalist W.S. Noble who himself became trapped by the advancing fires later wrote:

"Only those who have heard the heart-chilling roar of the racing fires with the booming of exploding clouds of gas know what a test of nerves, men, women and children passed through. It says something of the Australian character'.

A total of 69 sawmills were burnt to the ground claiming 71 lives. Over 1,000 homes were lost and the townships of Narbethong, Noojee, Woods Point, Nayook West and Hill End were destroyed.

Intense fires burned on the urban fringes of Melbourne around the Yarra Ranges, with large burning embers being carried for kilometres ahead of the main firefront.

The alpine towns of Bright, Cudgewa and Corryong were also affected, as were vast areas in the west between Portland, the Otway Ranges and the Grampians.

The intensity of the fires produced huge amounts of smoke with reports of ash falling as far away as New Zealand.

The devastation ended late on Sunday, January 15 after rain fell across the state. And three weeks after the rain, a Royal Commission was convened by Judge Leonard E.B. Stretton.

In his scathing 35-page report he attributed blame for the fires to careless burning, campfires, graziers, saw-millers and land clearing.

'The truth was hard to find ... much of the evidence was coloured by self-interest ... much of it was quite false... little of it was wholly truthful'.

While his recommendations led to sweeping changes to forest management others were never implemented after becoming bogged down by political bureaucracy.

However, his experience as a Royal Commissioner would be soon called upon again following another fire disaster.

This time his expertise would be drawn from, not only 'Black Friday,' but a tragic legacy of bushfires that already existed in Australia.

## 1851 — Black Thursday

On 6 February 1851, Victoria faced its first catastrophic bushfire.

It was the year Port Phillip District was elevated into the

colony of Victoria and its settlers watched in horror as the largest bushfire in European history broke out.

Records show it was the hottest day they could remember reaching 110 degrees Fahrenheit (43.3 degrees Celsius) in the shade. One report described 'a lurid sky' as would have existed 'during the destruction of Pompeii', while others feared 'it was the end of the world'.

Flames covered a quarter of the new state destroying one million sheep and thousands of head of cattle.

But remarkably, there were only 12 known deaths — owing no doubt to the relatively small population at the time.

## 1865 — Black Monday

Not since 'Black Thursday' had Victorians faced such fury as a single line of fire stretched from Geelong to Ballarat destroying everything in its path.

According to local press reports, 'Black Monday was the worst day for heat and smoke we have had since Black Thursday in 1851.

The destruction of property was very great, and no one who has not seen a fire raging among the stubbles and fences on tilled lands, with a strong north wind blowing, can well imagine what this is.'

## 1898 — Red Tuesday

Red Tuesday is another chapter in the resilience of early settlers facing the horrifying conflagration of Australian bushfires.

'Fires claimed 12 lives, destroyed over 2,000 buildings and affected about 15,000 people, leaving 2,500 homeless in the Cranbourne, Traralgon, Neerim South and Poowong areas' — Trove.

Stories of sensational yet pathetic attempts to take refuge in creeks and waterholes as a sea of flame swept down upon their townships.

Stories of bravery 'waiting in painful suspense lest the wind should change direction towards their homes'. And above all 'unswerving courage of men and women of the bush facing a wrath in its most horrifying shape, revealing striking examples of extraordinary resourcefulness in its presence'.

## 1926 — Black Sunday

Forest fires burnt across large areas of Gippsland throughout February and into early March.

The fires came to a peak on February 14, with 31 deaths recorded at Warburton while other areas affected include Noojee, Kinglake, Erica, and the Dandenong Ranges. Widespread fires also occurred across other eastern states.

A total of 60 lives were lost in addition to widespread damage to farms, homes and forests.

Then came the mother of all fires — Black Friday 1939.

## 1943/44 — WW2 Bushfires

The 1943 Victorian bushfire season began like so many others; in a severe drought. That summer was the driest ever recorded in Melbourne.

Between 22 December 1943 and 15 February 1944, 51 people

were killed, 700 injured, and 650 buildings were destroyed across the state.

Many personnel who would normally have been available to fight the fires had been posted overseas during World War II.

The first major fire was a grassfire at Wangaratta on 22 December which burnt hundreds of hectares and resulted in the deaths of 10 volunteer firefighters.

On 14 January and the following day, fires broke out across the state between the South Australian border and the outskirts of Geelong while another 9 deaths occurred in fires in the east around Morwell and Traralgon.

Close to Melbourne itself, 63 homes were destroyed at Beaumaris and Mentone while another 5 homes were destroyed at Pascoe Vale.

Before the smoke had even cleared, a blame game began and the public was demanding answers.

Premier Albert Dunstan decided to ask Judge Stretton to chair a second Royal Commission.

While the summer fires had claimed 51 lives it wasn't until the fire at Yallourn spread into the open-cut coalmine threatening Melbourne's electricity supplies that the Government was forced to act.

Stretton's new report again highlighted a lack of cohesive firefighting ability but directly led to the creation of the Country Fire Authority (CFA) in December 1944.

Internationally, the east coast of Australia is considered one of the three most fire-prone landscapes on Earth, however, as history also shows fires are indiscriminate and certainly not confined to Victoria.

## 1967 — Black Tuesday Tasmania

The Black Tuesday bushfires became the second-worst fire disaster in Australia and by far the worst Tasmania had ever endured.

In a span of 5 hours, 110 fires raged around southern Tasmania claiming 62 lives and leaving 900 injured. Fanned by 80 km/h winds one of the worst fire fronts came to within two kilometres of the centre of Hobart.

Other fires circled the city in a 52-kilometre radius destroying half a million acres of land leaving an estimated 62,000 farm animals dead and 7,000 people without homes. 80 bridges, 4,800 sections of power lines, 1,500 vehicles and over 100 other structures were destroyed leaving total damage amounting to $40 million.

## 2003 — Canberra fires

On 8 January 2003, a combination of extreme temperatures above 37oC, low humidity, and lightning strikes caused multiple bushfires to break out in the Kosciuszko and National parks surrounding Canberra.

On 18 January, two fire fronts combined to create a 25 km fire front and wind gusts of up to 65 km per hour propelled the fire towards Canberra.

A state of emergency was declared at 2:45 pm but by 3 pm the firestorm hit the outer streets of Duffy and soon reached the suburbs of Rivett, Chapman, Kambah, Higgins, Hawker and Cook. Four people were killed more than 435 people were injured and 5,000 were evacuated. There were approximately 488 houses destroyed leaving a total damage bill estimated at around $660 million.

Considered in terms of both losses of property and loss of life the 1939 bushfire was still one of the worst disasters, and certainly the worst bushfire event to have occurred in Australia up to that time.

But nothing prepared us for what was to come.

## Ash Wednesday
## – A personal perspective

1983 Ash Wednesday: "It was just a roar ...a constant, almost threatening sound... there was this enormous, enormous, noise, and it was fireballs flying ahead of the fire...the gates of hell were opened" — Survivors HSV7 News.

16 February 1983 began with PM Malcolm Fraser preparing his Liberal Party policy launch at the Malvern Town Hall. Two months earlier Fraser had opted for an early double dissolution. On the day he called the election, however, the ALP replaced its leader Bill Hayden with ACTU secretary Bob Hawke. The whole

political spectrum was thrown wide open. Hayden then claimed that a "drover's dog" could lead the ALP to victory. The drover's dog was now barking and the mood was as dark as the sky had been over Melbourne one week earlier when a huge disastrous dust storm swept in.

Since the dust storm and several bushfires around the state, a smoky haze had lingered in the air. To make matters worse, the day had dawned unexpectedly hot.

Shortly after midday the sky suddenly lost its dirty haze. The temperature had risen dramatically to 39 degrees and the humidity had fallen to an incredibly low 7 per cent. There was already an ominous feeling in the air but all eyes were on South Australia where bushfires were reportedly burning out of control.

By 3 pm the fire situation around Adelaide had worsened, highlighted on the radio by 5DN news reporter Murray Nichol who gave a graphic and emotional account of watching his own home being destroyed.

In Melbourne's Channel Seven newsroom, we began receiving reports of spotfires around Victoria but nothing abnormally large considering the weather conditions.

At 3:55 pm the temperature reached 43 degrees, the humidity was now down to 6 per cent and CFA headquarters in Malvern was reporting a fire at Belgrave on the outskirts of Melbourne. Shortly after 4 pm, the CFA confirmed the fire was "now out of control" and we urgently re-directed our news crew.

By now reports were filtering into all newsrooms of a sizeable dust storm approaching the city, which if it proved as big as last week, then would play havoc with helicopter transfers so close to our bulletins.

We had already dispatched the Channel Seven news chopper to cover a fire at Macedon; now we were forced to find another chopper to send to a fire in the Otway Ranges in the southeast.

The situation in South Australia was horrific with many reported killed and hundreds of homes destroyed. However, we were now facing our dilemma with no local vision from the Victorian fires being reported.

Another check with the CFA revealed the Belgrave fire was reaching major proportions and heading towards Narre Warren, east of Melbourne. Our news crew had been held up by a police roadblock.

Fires were also burning in Cockatoo, in the Otway's to the southeast and further west towards Warrnambool.

I left the newsroom chaos for a brief silent moment in the makeup department. As the unofficial policy went, 'no pictures no story'. Priority, I believed, would be given to the Adelaide fires where at least we could see some flames. As the news anchor with just two minutes to go, I then rushed into the studio still unaware of the lead story.

Then panic took over. I had no scripts, no pictures and no advice on what to do. One minute to go. The producer burst into the heavy soundproof doors and ran across the studio floor, thrusting a handful of papers at me. The floor manager had already begun the final countdown calling 'five seconds to go'. The theme began as I heard, 'Mal, read the top one. Read the top one.'

'Cue, Mal.'

'Good evening...'

Just a few minutes earlier, the link van had begun feeding footage of the Belgrave fire into the ENG communication centre where editors had rush-cut and edited our first story at the last moment.

Unaware of developments, confusion continued on the studio floor. As I was reading the second story, news staff were rushing in handing me updates.

One fire was out of control and heading towards Upper Beaconsfield another outbreak was roaring through the Otway Ranges to the south while more serious reports were coming in from other parts of Victoria.

I became lost in a mountain of paper. The second film story suddenly ended, cutting back to me at the desk sorting through piles of scripts and phoning the producer for advice.

'Forgive me for a moment,' I said as I shuffled the sheets, 'the news reports are coming in faster than I can read them'.

I suppose it added to the drama but there was now no disguising the awful truth. The viewers could only surmise the state was in the grip of an awesome crisis, second only to the one that was unfolding in our television studio.

As the hazy sun rose over the city the following morning, Melbourne awoke in a state of shock. No one was untouched. Cinders had fallen on the city, and towns had been destroyed. Seventy-two people died in those 24 hours. The Victorian towns of Gisborne, Upper Beaconsfield, Framlingham, Naringal, Narre Warren, Cockatoo and Macedon were extensively damaged.

While fires formed a semi-circle around Melbourne, others fires raged through the heavily populated coastal areas west of Warrnambool. In one of the worst incidents, 12 firefighters at Beaconsfield became trapped and perished in their tanker. In the same area, police found one man dead in his farmhouse still clutching a hose across his chest. His wife lay dead two metres away.

What is regarded as one of Australia's major natural disasters can also be attributed to a man-made disaster; caused in part by broken power lines and made worse by reports that some of the fires were deliberately lit.

Excerpts from Mal Walden's memoir 'The Newsman".

# Shipwrecks
# — High Seas Heroes

**Heroes on High Seas**

'The screams from passengers who had fallen to their knees in prayer were lost to the sound of the storm that raged above. As each wave struck their vessel it rose, then fell to the bottom of a giant trough before rising again to repeat the terrifying ordeal. Wooden joists creaked under strain as the foaming torrents that had battered the decks, ripping sheets and topsails above, then flooded down to the vomit and the hell below. Rising and falling, rolling and twisting, with desperate crews manning bilge pumps, often the last defence for hope and salvation'.

Extracts from National Archives

The 'Hell on the High Seas' was experienced by many early settlers seeking a new life in Australia. Many didn't make it, falling victim to the savage elements at sea or uncharted reefs along an unwelcome coast.

Documented stories by those who did survive form a lasting tribute to Australia's maritime heroes.

> *'The sky blackened, the wind arose and in half an hour more it blew a perfect hurricane, accompanied with thunder, lightning and rain... I never before saw a sea in such a rage... Most were down on their knees in prayer –*
> **Arthur Bowes Smith — Surgeon**

Any land 'girt by sea' is reliant on shipping and during those early years of settlement, the journey by sea was long and dangerous.

In calm weather, a sailing ship from Europe took up to four months to complete the journey, while a well-run clipper with favourable winds could make it in a little over half that time.

By the 1850s it was possible to travel by auxiliary steamer, using a combination of steam and sail. But for most, life at sea was uncomfortable and often hazardous, particularly for passengers who travelled cheaply in 'steerage' (the lowest deck and below the waterline).

The spread of disease and death from illness was only one of the risks. Deaths at sea were tragically common with as many as one in five children and one in 60 adults failing to survive the voyage to Australia.

Storms were also common and a disaster at sea left little hope for rescue as few sailors or passengers could swim and there were rarely enough lifeboats for the numbers on board.

But an even greater danger lay ahead. The rocky coastlines and uncharted waters would claim many vessels and many lives.

## The Cataraqui — 1845

The sinking of the Cataraqui is considered Australia's worst-ever civil maritime disaster. The British barque departed from Liverpool on the 20th of April 1845 carrying 411 people, comprising 367 emigrants, many of them women and children travelling in family groups, and 44 crew. During its voyage, one crew member was lost overboard, six people died and five babies were born, leaving a total of 409 people on board. King Island Bass Strait had become a popular shortcut for shipping between England and Sydney saving around a week by avoiding a circumnavigation of Tasmania. But at 4:30 am on Monday 4 August 1845, in stormy weather, the Cataraqui struck a reef on the west coast of King Island less than 100 metres from shore.

Around 300 passengers reacted by climbing onto the deck where large waves immediately washed many out to sea. Half an hour later, the ship listed to its port side, and passengers cowering below decks drowned as the ship filled with water.

The following morning, some 200 surviving passengers and crew still clung onto the deck, but at 4 pm the ship broke in two tossing another 100 survivors into the turbulent waters. The crew then tried to provide a lifeline to the shore when they launched a buoy attached to a rope, but it became caught in kelp. At 5 pm, the wreck further disintegrated, leaving around 70 survivors clutching the bow. The crew launched another small boat, but it capsized in the wild conditions, drowning all six on board.

There were only nine survivors — one passenger, Solomon Brown, and eight crew. 400 passengers and crew perished. The disaster may have been Australia's worst but it wasn't the first.

## Tryall — 1662

The Tryall was a British East India Company-owned ship launched in 1621.

She was under the command of John Brooke en route from Cape Town to Batam in the East Indies when it struck rocks and sank off the West Australian coast.

Her crew are believed to have been the first Englishmen to sight Australia 108 years before Captain Cook.

She had stopped at Cape Town for supplies on 19 March 1622 and loaded its cargo including silver for trade as well as a gift for the King of Siam.

However, after her departure, she encountered a navigational error that caused her to have sailed too far east.

Finally, the winds turned to favourable south-westerlies and they started to make good progress towards their destination of Batavia.

On the morning of 25 May 1662, she struck uncharted submerged rocks about 32 kilometres northwest of the outer edge of the Montebello Island group.

Captain Brooke, his son John and nine men scrambled into a skiff while 35 others managed to save themselves in a longboat.

Brooke sailed separately to Java while the crew spent seven days ashore on the Montebello Islands, before sailing the longboat to Batam in Java.

The skiff arrived at Batavia on 5 July 1622 and the longboat three days later — a voyage of over 1,800 kilometres.

Of the 143 men who had left England, 93 had perished at the

scene of the wreck and one person died in the skiff in what is today regarded as the first recorded shipwreck in Australia's history.

## The Zuytdorp — 1711

On 1 August 1711 Zuytdorp (meaning 'South village') was dispatched from the Netherlands. It was reported to be holding a load of freshly minted silver coins to take to the trading port of Batavia, now Jakarta, Indonesia. It never arrived at its destination. No search was undertaken since there was no idea where the ship was lost. The crew were never heard from again.

In 1834, Aborigines near the recently colonised settlement of Perth reported wreckage some distance to the North and coins discovered on the beach. However, local officials presumed it was a recent wreck and having sent rescue parties they failed to find any survivors or their remains.

In 1927 more wreckage, including coins (some dated 1711), bottle fragments, timbers including a spar, a carved female figure, breech blocks from swivel guns and other objects including evidence of a deliberately lit fire, were discovered at the foot of cliffs around the same location.

It's now believed the relics strongly point to the disappearance of the Zuytdorp which may have sunk during a violent storm in 1711 with the loss of 286 lives.

## The Neva — 1835

Neva was a three-masted barque launched in 1813. She made two voyages transporting convicts to Australia. It was on her second voyage in 1835 that tragedy struck.

Neva had sailed from Cork in Ireland on 8 January 1835, carrying 150 female convicts and their 33 children, together with nine free women (probable wives of convicts) and their 22 children. There were 26 crew under the command of Captain Benjamin Peck. With the deaths of a crewman, a convict and a free woman, and one birth, during the voyage, by the time she reached the Australian coastline Neva's total complement was 239.

At about 5 am on 13, May 1835 Neva hit an uncharted reef northwest of King Island in the Bass Strait and immediately broke up. Many of the women became hopelessly drunk on rum being carried as cargo and were unable to save themselves.

Twenty-two survivors drifted ashore on the northern end of King Island on two rafts formed by the fore and aft decks of the collapsed ship.

The remaining fifteen survivors, including the captain and the chief officer, lived with local sealer John Scott and his aboriginal wives and children until a fortnight later when the schooner Sarah Ann rescued them and carried them safely to Launceston.

Neva is recorded as one of the worst shipwrecks in Australia's history with the loss of 244 lives.

## The Dunbar — 1854

The Dunbar launched on 30 November 1854 was one of several large sailing ships that began trading with Australia as a result of the Australian gold rushes.

The Dunbar was built as a first-class passenger and cargo carrier rigged and well-fitted out as the largest timber vessel constructed in Sunderland. This was partly in response to the demand for ships to carry passengers to the Australian goldfields.

On the night of 20 August 1857, the ship approached the entrance to Port Jackson NSW from the south, but heavy rain and strong gale-force winds made navigating difficult. The ship's captain, James Green, either erroneously believing he had already passed the harbour's southern headland or mistaking a smaller break in the coastline known as The Gap, drove the ship onto rocks.

There were 59 crew and 63 passengers on board as it rapidly broke apart. Only one out of a total complement of 122 survived. While bodies and wreckage filled the harbour, Able Seaman James Johnson, managed to cling to the cliff face until finally rescued many hours later.

James Johnson was eventually employed in Newcastle as an assistant lighthouse keeper and on 12 July 1866, was instrumental in rescuing the sole survivor of the paddle steamer SS Cawarra 12 years later.

## SS Cawarra — 1866

The SS Cawarra was a Brisbane-bound passenger-carrying paddle steamer owned by the Australasian Steamship Company.

On 12 July 1866, she became caught in rough seas along the NSW coast. The storm wreaked havoc sinking 14 other ships and resulting in 77 deaths between Port Stephens in the north and Sydney to the south.

As the Cawarra entered Newcastle harbour to take shelter it was overwhelmed by huge waves and sank, bow first, before thousands of onlookers who had gathered along the harbour shoreline to watch in horror. There was little they could do to help in such horrendous conditions.

Several hours later, the lighthouse keeper sighted a survivor and with his assistant, James Johnson, who had been the sole survivor of the Dunbar wreck, launched a boat and brought the man ashore.

Ordinary seaman Frederick Hedges had grabbed a plank as the ship sank and was eventually washed more dead than alive against a harbour buoy. He was the sole survivor of 60 passengers who lost their lives on the Cawarra.

## Loch Ard — 1878

The Loch Ard was launched in 1863 as one of the last generations of fast sailing vessels known as clippers, designed to compete with the speed of the steamships.

She had endured a chequered life before her final voyage. She twice lost her masts rounding Ireland and India and was almost driven ashore at Sorrento, Victoria. On another voyage, the captain died and the ship nearly ran aground on the way to Calcutta.

However, her legacy would leave 52 dead, and a miraculous tale of survival to become one of Australia's most famous shipwrecks.

Loch Ard's final voyage began on March 2, 1878. from Gravesend, bound for Melbourne, under the command of Captain George Gibb.

The ship was carrying cargo that included building materials, copper, marble fireplaces, gaslight fittings, lead, railway iron, cement, confectionery, clocks and objects intended for display at the 1880 International Exhibition in Melbourne, including a large porcelain peacock.

Just days from its destination, the Loch Ard entered Bass Strait. Captain Gibb stood anxiously waiting for the welcoming flash of the Cape Otway light but with fog and sea hindering his view, it was only minutes before the ominous cliff and breakers suddenly loomed.

Desperate attempts to alter course failed, and despite turning the bow out to sea, the Loch Ard struck Mutton Bird Island.

The crash brought down the masts, crushing passengers who had made their way on deck and making it difficult to launch lifeboats. The ship sank within about 15 minutes.

Of the 54 people on board only two survived, passenger Eva Carmichael, and crewman Tom Pearce both of whom became celebrity legends in their lifetime and beyond.

## Quetta — 1890

RMS Quetta was a Royal Mail Ship that plied the North Queensland coast in the 1880s.

The ship was initially designed for 72 saloons (first class) and 32 steerage (second class) passengers.

On the night of 28 February 1890, the ship turned into the Adolphus Channel to round Cape York Peninsular. The pilot was experienced, the weather fine and visibility good, but at 9:14 pm the ship struck an uncharted rock in the middle of the channel.

At the time of the disaster, Quetta had 292 people aboard including a crew of 121.

The rock ripped a hole through the plates from the bow to the engine room amidships, four to 12 feet wide, sinking Quetta in 5 minutes and sending 134 of her passengers to their deaths. Of those thrown into the water, many were sucked down in the vortex, making it one of Queensland's biggest maritime disasters.

## Missing Football team — 1892

Described as one of the worst sporting team accidents the world had seen 15 young men, including 14 local football players, drowned when their boat capsized off the Victorian Peninsula town of Mornington on 21 May 1892.

It's believed a freak storm struck their boat as the Mornington team returned from a game at Mordialloc. Several others had taken the train.

All onboard the yacht 'Process' perished, including 13-year-old Charles Hooper, who was crewing for his father, the skipper, so no one knows exactly what happened.

But there were chilling clues, such as the hull scratches, noticed when the boat was found, half-submerged, off Mt Eliza the next day as each boy desperately tried to stay afloat.

It's believed the severe squall snapped wires connecting the masts and sails to the boat keeling it over and tossing its occupants overboard.

Unsecured ballast stones are thought to have slid into one end of the hull, making the boat too heavy to re-float.

Clothing found washed ashore suggested players had shed their gear to avoid sinking as they clung to each other in the frigid water.

The drownings devastated the 800 close-knit Victorian community of Mornington.

## Yongala — 1911

The SS Yongala, which sank off the Queensland coast on 23 March 1911 took the lives of all 122 passengers and crew.

In March of that year, the steel-hulled passenger and freight steamer embarked on her 99th voyage in Australian waters. She left

Melbourne with 72 passengers, heading for Brisbane, Townsville and Cairns picking up new passengers at Brisbane and MacKay.

Five hours after leaving Mackay, the lighthouse keeper at Dent Island saw the Yongala sail into the Whitsunday Passage. This would be the last known sighting of the ship.

Shortly before the vessel left sight of land, a telegram was received by the Flat Top signal station warning of a tropical cyclone between Townsville and Mackay.

Flag and wireless signals from the station prompted several ships to take refuge at Mackay, but Yongala did not see the flags and was yet to be fitted with wireless equipment.

At the time, she had 122 people on board, as well as cargo, and a racehorse named Moonshine.

At first, no one noticed that she was missing, since it was assumed she had taken refuge in the Whitsunday Islands to wait out the storm. But by March 26, after she was due at her final destination, it was posted that she was missing.

Several days later, cargo washed up on the shores east of Townsville which identified it as from the SS Yongala. But there were no signs of survivors.

Her fate remained a mystery for 50 years until she was finally found in 1958, 30 metres below the surface off Cape Bowling Green near Townsville.

To this day the only body recovered was that of the racehorse, Moonshine.

## HMAS Sydney — 1941

On 19 November 1941, HMAS Sydney, a light cruiser of the Royal Australian Navy with an impressive record of war service, was lost following a battle with the German raider Kormoran in the Indian

Ocean off the Western Australian coast.

For 12 days the government maintained the strictest secrecy about the loss of Sydney. When Prime Minister John Curtin made the first of two public announcements on 1 December 1941, he did little more than confirm rumours that Sydney had been sunk.

For the public, the shock of the loss was accompanied by the anger that information was being concealed.

Little information was released until 1957 when the official history of the RAN in World War II was published.

HMAS Sydney had celebrated successful battles in the Mediterranean, where she famously sank the Italian cruiser Bartolomeo Colleoni. Her crew of predominantly young men received a hero's welcome on their return to Australia in February 1941.

She was then tasked with escorting troopships to Southeast Asia, following an Indian Ocean route along the coast of Western Australia. It was on the return of one of these voyages that she encountered the HSK Kormoran, on 19 November 1941.

When the Australian ship asked the Kormoran to identify itself, the German ship responded that it was a merchant ship with cargo.

After several minutes of not responding to further questioning, the German ship suddenly revealed its true identity and shots were fired from both ships almost simultaneously.

The intense fire continued for 30 minutes, at the end of which, both ships had caught fire and were badly damaged.

All 645 crew members onboard Sydney were killed when the ship sank.

Of the 399 onboard the Kormoran, 82 were killed and 317 were captured.

In total, 727 lives were lost in this disaster.

For almost seven decades, the final resting place of Sydney and her crew remained unknown.

In mid-March 2008 the Australian Government announced that the wreckages of both Sydney and Kormoran had been found, approximately 112 nautical miles off Steep Point, Western Australia.

## Melbourne–Voyager collision — 1964

On the evening of 10 February 1964, the two ships, aircraft carrier HMAS Melbourne and HMAS Voyager a destroyer escort were performing manoeuvres off the NSW coast near Jervis Bay.

Melbourne's aircraft were performing flying exercises, and Voyager was tasked in guard position behind and to the left of the carrier.

After a series of manoeuvrers, the two ships ended with Voyager ahead and to the right of the carrier. The destroyer was then ordered to resume plane guard position, which would involve turning to starboard, away from the carrier, then looping around behind. Instead, Voyager began a starboard turn but then came around to port. The bridge crew on Melbourne assumed that Voyager was moving to allow the carrier to overtake her.

Senior personnel on Voyager were not paying attention to the manoeuvre. At 10:55 pm officers on both ships began desperate manoeuvres to avoid a collision. But by then it was too late.

Melbourne struck Voyager with the carrier's bow striking just behind the bridge and cutting the destroyer in two.

Of the 314 aboard Voyager, 82 were killed, most of whom died immediately or were trapped in the heavy bow section, which sank within 10 minutes. The rest of the ship sank after midnight.

Melbourne, although damaged, suffered no fatalities, and was able to sail to Sydney the next morning with most of the Voyager survivors aboard — the rest had been taken to the naval base, HMAS Creswell.

## Sydney to Hobart yacht race — 1998

Of the 115 yachts that set sail from Sydney Harbour on 26 December 1998, only 44 reached their destination in Hobart.

It would become the most disastrous in the blue water classic's history, with the loss of six lives.

The cause of this disaster was an intense low-pressure system that began forming in the Bass Strait before the race started.

On the 2nd day of the race, severe weather conditions struck the fleet off the south-eastern Australian coast. The weather system then built into an exceptionally strong storm with winds gusting to 80 knots. The rising storm caused the sinking of five boats, seven were abandoned and 55 sailors had to be rescued from their yachts by ships and helicopters in the largest peacetime search and rescue effort ever seen in Australia.

## Blythe Heroes

On the evening of October 12, 1973, the typical post-war coastal freighter, Blythe Star, slipped its moorings from Prince of Wales Bay, Hobart, for a routine two-day voyage north to King Island. Her ten-man crew was charged with carrying a full cargo — 350 tonnes of bagged superphosphate fertiliser and a tonne of kegged beer — stowed in the hold and lashed to the deck.

This was to be the ship's tragic final voyage. Three crew would die, a botched rescue would unfold and heroes would emerge to tell of a tragedy that changed the course of maritime safety.

By 5:15 am on Saturday, the lighthouse keeper on duty at Maatsuyker Island logged a small, grey, tanker-like freighter making its way westwards, though he was unable to read its name.

Shortly before 8 am, a crew member noticed that the ship had developed a slight list to starboard. So too did the chief engineer, John Eagles, who rushed up to the bridge to ask the captain what was going on. The captain said he didn't know, but that the list seemed to be righting itself. The chief went below to check if any of the tanks had taken water. Moments later the ship suddenly lurched to starboard, rolling 90 degrees. Water was now pouring in over the side and into the stricken vessel.

The crew quickly scrambled aft to where the bosun was launching the rubber life raft. Eagles managed to kill the engine as they all leapt to relative safety. Within 10 minutes of the first alert, the Blythe Star gave a great hiss and sank stern first. All 10 crew had escaped with little more than a few cuts and bruises although some were dressed only in knickers and sox.

However, their euphoria at surviving was cut short when Captain Cruickshank informed them he had been unable to send off an SOS radio message or had brought the emergency portable radio with him.

For eight days they drifted more than 400km along the south and east coasts of Tasmania, at the mercy of the strong winds and currents. One night a huge storm struck the raft, collapsing in on the freezing occupants, and forcing them to bail for their lives.

On the fourth day, the second engineer John Sloan died after suffering a medical condition and was eventually given a sea burial.

In the meantime, they saw no signs of any major search.

The men were unaware a search had started slowly and was marked by guesswork and bureaucratic bumbling. The boat was last seen by the lighthouse keeper — but his report was ignored.

The alert was not raised until two days after the ship went down.

There was a further complication: all ships leaving Hobart and heading north had a choice of which side of Tasmania they planned to sail. The Blythe Star had not communicated to authorities which course they would take.

Despite the most extensive air-sea search in Australia at the time, no trace of the vessel was found. Compounding the problem aircraft from the RAAF base at Sale were tasked to search the entire coast of Tasmania instead of being concentrated in the south and west.

Meanwhile, the men were surviving on glucose powder and just 50ml of tinned water a day as sharks continued to circle their flimsy raft.

On day eight of their ordeal, they drifted into Deep Glen Bay on the remote Forestier Peninsula. But high cliffs hindered their escape and two crewmen badly hurt in falls died from exhaustion and hypothermia.

Realising all would perish unless they found help, the young deckhand, 18-year-old Michael Doleman, led two men up the cliffs and then spent a day and night wandering through an almost impenetrable forest until they stumbled on a forestry worker and were taken to the nearest township. A rescue helicopter picked up their mates.

It was then they learnt the search had been called off the previous day as they had been given up for dead.

The Blythe Star has never been found and what caused the ship to capsize is still a mystery. The most likely cause was the ship's chief engineer mistakenly emptying a ballast tank. With nothing to counterbalance the sudden shift of weight, the ship rolled violently onto her right side and sank.

A court of inquiry found virtually none of those involved in the vessel's operations, or in the search that commenced after she was reported missing, escaped criticism.

Three men died after the Blythe Star capsized: Kenneth Jones, John Sloane and John Eagles. Their suffering, and that of the men who survived, was not entirely in vain.

The subsequent Marine Board of Inquiry contributed to the establishment of a ship reporting system. The AusRep system now ensures mariners regularly report their routes to authorities and all life rafts are fitted with radio beacons.

In 2016, Michael Doleman, the last living survivor of Blythe Star spoke publicly for the first time in 42 years.

He was the irrepressible 18-year-old deckhand at the time — the son of a seafarer who hailed from Doveton, Melbourne with just two years of sailing experience when disaster struck.

"The three lives of my comrades were a hell of a high price to pay for this, but there are seafarers alive today because of the changes," Doleman said. "They didn't lose their lives in vain."

A few months later Doleman retired as deputy national secretary of the Maritime Union of Australia denying he had ever been a hero but having dedicated his career to improving marine safety for all.

The Australian National Maritime Museum

*"One who conquers the sea today is ready to conquer the ocean tomorrow."*
*Matshona Dhliwayo*

*Thanks to Joelle Gergis — Australian National University, ABC Broadcasting, Victorian Maritime Centre, A Hell on High Seas.*

# Cyclones and a personal story from Darwin

'The wind built to a high-pitched shriek with a low-frequency rumble... constant thumps, as trees and household wreckage struck our home... screeching as our roof peeled off ... the walls shaking violently until they fell apart at the seams...'

'Then deadly silence... distant cries for help... before it struck with even greater force from the opposite direction'.

Quotes from survivors I interviewed for HSV7's 6:30 pm News, Boxing Day 1974.

## First Impressions, Darwin 1974

*'Apocalypse'. 'Catastrophe'. 'Devastation'!*
If I was to be truly accurate my first words were 'Holy shit!'

Darwin appeared through the window of our charted Lear jet as we descended through thick clouds on Boxing Day morning.

It was a surreal black and white image, sepia at best in the early dawn light, and very like the photos, I had seen of post-war Hiroshima and Nagasaki. Suburb after suburb was flattened beyond recognition. Streets were vaguely outlined but homes and buildings had been laid waste and scattered for as far as the eye could see. The "eye" in this case, more than 20 kilometres wide, had passed directly over the city and nothing in its path had been spared.

Even houses that miraculously were still standing had been left uninhabitable. However, the sight from above could not have prepared us for the tragedy unfolding below with 71 people dead.

The runway had been cleared of wreckage and as we touched down, aircraft lay scattered on each side of the strip, like toys discarded in a toddler's tantrum. Planes of all shapes and sizes had been tossed at random; some lay crumpled beneath damaged hangers while others lay where they rested intact but contorted at odd angles. We stepped from the comfort zone of our pressurised cabin into a humid atmosphere of unbearable heartache amid an omnipresent sense of tragedy you could see, feel and smell.

Two army privates who had survived in the nearby barracks stopped. They invited us to join them on their way to inspect their own home in one of the worst-hit suburbs of Nightcliff. Most roads were blocked by indistinguishable wreckage and we passed many residents searching through the remains of their homes. Some called for help and were advised to make their way to the airport while we continued our journey.

Several moments later a dog ran out in front of our vehicle trailing a partly severed leg. We braked and swerved. I looked back as a man emerged carrying a large piece of wood, which he raised above the dog's head. I looked away, already knowing its fate. No one spoke. Trees were dismembered, stripped of foliage and each wrapped tightly by roofing iron-like tourniquets squeezing out what little life was left. And there was little life left. No insects. No birds just an eerie silence and a pungent odour of decay which was already beginning to pervade the area.

We eventually arrived at the army boys' apartment to find the doors missing and a fridge lying on its side having spewed its contents from the kitchen to the bedroom. Most furniture and appliances were scattered, broken or simply blown away. Curtains were shredded, windows smashed and everything soaked in water. The boys kicked a broken television and just stood and wept. A neighbour arrived to offer sympathy and then proceeded to describe how he had survived with his wife and two children.

'A loud explosion signalled the whole side of our home had been torn away.' 'Then a rending screech above as the roof peeled away' and with it went the washing machine and the kitchen stove with the same ease of force that had already sucked all the Christmas decorations from their home.

The boys then stopped crying, realising after a night like that survival was all that mattered.

## Christmas morning 1974

Like most Australians, I awoke on Christmas morning in 1974 to sketchy reports that Cyclone Tracy had struck Darwin. Damage unknown. Communications down. Nothing was confirmed.

She blew in just after midnight and despite warnings on local radio, it caught many sceptical Territorians by surprise. The wind continued to increase until 3:05 am when the anemometer at the airport recorded gusts of 217 km/h before it broke. Estimates have since put those gusts at 250 km/h.

As it moved across the city and suburbs it gave its victims a brief respite. Twenty minutes of silence from its roar and screams.

Tracy teased the Territorians with a false sense of survival. Just when they felt it was safe to emerge from their damaged homes, she struck again with even greater force. This time the winds came from the opposite direction. Tracy left no part of the city untouched. Ninety per cent of all buildings were destroyed or left uninhabitable. As families huddled together in cupboards, under beds, in bathrooms and particularly toilets (the smallest and safest room in the house), the rest of Australia slept in glorious oblivion.

We were aware that General Alan Stretton, head of the newly formed Natural Disasters Organisation (NDO), was being dispatched from Canberra.

General Stretton had been awake since a 6:20 am phone call from the Cyclone Tropical Warning Centre in Perth. Darwin had been hit but no further details were available. That single phone call triggered the start of the most massive relief operation in Australia's history. Just by chance, Stretton found a phone number for the Darwin police station and rang direct. The officer on duty, Sergeant Taylor, reported that the roof of the hospital had blown off leaving several unidentified bodies. It was only 5 am so no vehicle had been able to leave the station to assess the damage. That was the last call into Darwin before all communications went down. It was all Stretton needed to mobilise his organisation. He would later write:

It was unbelievable that the defence forces with all the millions of dollars spent on signals equipment could not communicate with their units in Darwin. What if there had been an enemy attack?

It wasn't until 10 am EST that the Marine Operations Centre received a sketchy communication in Morse code from the MV Nyanda, which had just entered Darwin harbour after riding out the storm at sea. The only other message out of Darwin came through the offices of the Overseas Telecommunications Centre at the airport, which reported massive devastation and the terminal filling with refugees. Then they too went off the air.

In Canberra, General Stretton began by organising medical supplies, stretchers, field cooking equipment, refrigerators and tarpaulins, 200,000 rations had been ordered, enough to feed the population for four to five days.

## Christmas Day 1974 — 3:18 P.M.

Early afternoon on Christmas Day two aircraft took off bound for Darwin. As our chartered Lear jet roared into the Melbourne sky, a RAAF VIP BAC111 was taking off from Canberra. Aboard that flight was General Alan Stretton, a team of medical staff with supplies and one ABC junior cameraman who had hitched a lift at the last moment. Aboard our flight were two pilots, one of our most experienced senior cameramen, Mike Meahan, his assistant Loz Bowie , two journalists from the Herald Sun to help share costs and me, the cadet TV reporter desperate to save his job.

As we broke through clouds and turned into the mid-afternoon sun on a heading for Alice Springs, the RAAF BAC111 was en route to Mackay to pick up the Minister for the Northern Territory, Dr Rex Patterson. They would later transfer to a Hercules at Mt Isa, which they believed would be better suited for an emergency landing in Darwin if it was found to be necessary. It was during the final leg of their flight that acting PM Jim Cairns contacted Stretton by radio giving him "supreme authority". Stretton would later concede, 'I knew the power was essentially of a de facto nature and could have no legal basis.' He, therefore, decided to rely on the bluff.

Less than ten minutes out of Darwin, the turbulence struck. Not as severe as we were expecting. Suddenly the dark grey skies became lighter as we dropped beneath the heavier clouds giving us our first sight of the carnage below. It was raining as dawn broke on this new day.

There was little skill in finding the story. Everywhere the camera pointed, there was devastation. Everyone we spoke to had a remarkable story of survival to tell.

Within less than an hour, we shot several rolls of film. The problem we would face was over-shooting. After our first interviews, we made our way to the airport where I renewed my acquaintance with General Alan Stretton. He gave an immediate assessment of the damage and shocked us when he announced, 'I'm going to evacuate this city beginning immediately.' He then likened the scene of devastation to Hiroshima and several times during our interview became visibly close to tears. In the end, he asked me what I was going to do with the interview and I told him it would be flown back to Melbourne on our plane.

'No, young man, I am the supreme commander here and I am commandeering every aircraft able to fly. The only time yours will take off is when it's full of evacuees.'

I ran through the crowd at the airport terminal calling out, 'Anyone wanting to go to Melbourne raise your hands.'

Within two minutes I had picked out ten evacuees fit enough to travel and located Stretton again for his official clearance.

## Boxing Day 1974 — 7:58 A.M.

Two hours and twenty-three minutes after landing in Darwin, I stood with the camera crew and watched as our Lear jet screamed down the rain-soaked runway and roared into the misty sky carrying the first two canisters of film the world would see of Cyclone Tracy's destruction of Darwin. It then began to rain again.

While Stretton was setting out his priorities, we set about organising ours. We began by heading in the direction of the Travelodge Motel, which stood as a symbol of survival above a skyline that lay devastated beneath it. The foyer was scattered with hastily packed suitcases.

Small groups gathered for evacuation after spending the night huddled in basements and the dining room. It already smelt of stale tropical mildew. The pool contained at least one car and debris was scattered around the grounds but apart from that, the hotel remained fairly intact. Many of its windows had blown out but one room on the fifth floor was habitable. The one requirement was to bucket our water up the stairs to flush the toilet. Dry camp stretchers were brought in and the one broken window was sealed.

The relief operation was now in full swing.

While supplies were being unloaded from the Hercules that had touched down moments before we arrived, General Stretton was convincing local authorities that he had the authorisation to take charge and no one questioned him. Priorities were food, water, local transport, searching for bodies and of course the massive task of evacuation. Of the 47,000 inhabitants, he decided to immediately reduce the number by 10,000.

That afternoon acting PM Jim Cairns and his wife Gwen arrived and we joined the cavalcade of local dignitaries and a growing band of media as they toured the worst parts. Not that there were any better parts. They both became visibly upset and Mrs Cairns broke down in tears on several occasions. At the end of the day, Stretton called a media conference on the steps of the police station.

It was followed by a broadcast on ABC radio, which by then was back on the air. As dusk quickly descended we drove back out to the airport to find a pilot on one of the many relief planes that would fly our film back to Melbourne.

## Friday 27 December 1974

The day began with another press conference during which Stretton pledged at all times to be honest with the media. There was already much speculation on the death toll and rumours that the true figure was being downplayed. This he assured us was nonsense. Dignitaries from all around Australia were now on their way. Politicians, union leaders, and state leaders; all eager to be seen and shown to be offering support.

He also praised the media which was slowly gathering into a huge international force. The media he said was generating nationwide sympathy and support. We were unaware of any feedback as communication to our respective newsrooms was unavailable and any phone calls in those first few days were restricted to emergency calls only.

The body count had now reached 47 and the temperature was over 40 degrees. Stray dogs were being rounded up and shot and the decaying stench was getting worse by the day raising further health fears. We were now concentrating on human-interest stories with survivors who were telling amazing stories of clinging to what was left of their homes to stay alive.

Keith Jessop was one such man who had survived the cyclone of 1937, the Japanese attack in 1942 and now Tracy.

He described his terrifying survival. 'There was just me and my wife ... huddling under our bed until the room filled with water.' Then as the water rose we struggled to reach a wardrobe for support,'... moments later the whole ceiling crashed in on us.'

Others described moving from room to room as each one disintegrated around them. One story revealed how a mother grabbed her daughter's legs to prevent her from being blown away. There was also a wife who found her decapitated husband during those silent moments in the eye of the storm but couldn't remember how she survived when the eye passed and the storm returned. Some were asphyxiated by the pressure from Cyclone Tracy, leaving bodies intact. The horrors were told in graphic detail, as survivors seemed keen to talk about their ordeals before they invariably broke down on camera. As we moved from one scene to the next, each story continued to break down our own emotions affecting our ability to operate as a news crew.

PM Gough Whitlam had flown in from Greece that day and after his press conference, we then drove back out to the airport to find another pilot to send our story back to Melbourne. In ten days, we never lost one report thanks to the pilots we had entrusted to carry our film.

## Sunday 29 December 1974

Stretton was now negotiating with the unions to get them onside for wharf duties in time for the arrival of the fleet. The evacuation had reached its peak of 8,000 in one day with the population now down to 16,000. The strain was now showing on Stretton. During one of his regular trips through the suburbs with the media in tow, a woman emerged to offer him a ripe mango.

'It is a gift for you,' she said. A gift she had saved to give him personally. He broke down and wept.

As we followed through the streets of Parap he stopped again when he caught sight of movement in a wrecked house. Emerging from the ruins stepped a man, his wife and two young children. They had been huddling there together, a family in shock since Christmas Eve when Tracy struck. Four days in the ruins with two children aged four and 18 months. With cameras rolling the media throng pushed closer as Stretton introduced himself to the father who then broke down.

'I have lost everything,' he cried, 'I have now no reason to live.'

We all cried at that moment. There was not a dry eye among the entire media contingent. The distraught husband's name was Sam who became a symbol of Darwin's survivors and the lead story around Australia once it was filed. Sam was originally from Syria so General Stretton arranged for his children to be flown back to Damascus until his house had been rebuilt.

Six months later, Stretton took his wife back to Darwin where they paid a visit to Sam and his family who had moved back to their new home.

By now some journalists had dubbed Stretton the "Weeping Dictator" and the "Johnny Ray of Generals". His nightly press conferences invariably started "off the record" and ended in tears.

## Monday 30 December 1974

The day started quietly enough, although by now it was becoming more difficult to find new angles and new stories. We were only waiting in Darwin for the fleet to arrive in several days and for General Stretton to hand over his powers and leave.

We then decided to see if there were any stories from the courthouse opposite the police station. There had been talk of looting and charges pending.

The court we chose happened to be hearing a case against an Aboriginal man charged with obtaining whisky by impersonating a police officer. Those charges alone appeared disturbing, as the man who stood in the dock resembled anything but a police officer. He was grubby, bearded, longhaired, wearing tattered shorts and a dirty T-shirt. If there was one thing he could never have been accused of, it was impersonating a police officer. There were no Aboriginal persons in the NT Police Force at the time. Magistrate David McCann sentenced him to nine months of hard labour, at which point we left the court. I then spotted Stretton at the police station and immediately rushed up to ask him whether the sentence could be interpreted as racial discrimination.

'Okay boys,' he said, 'roll that camera.' And on cue, he ran across the street and up the steps of the courthouse until stopped by an officer of the court.

'Don't you know who I am?' he barked.

'I know who you are sir,' the young officer replied, 'but you have no authority over this court.'

Stretton backed off momentarily then continued. 'I demand to see the Magistrate.'

A moment later McCann emerged to investigate the shouting. Suddenly he saw our camera and became very angry. Stretton called on us to stop filming explaining he would meet us on the steps shortly.

An hour later he appeared with his arm around McCann and apologised for any discourtesy he may have shown. However, we no longer had an exclusive story.

The word quickly spread and a large media contingent had now gathered before adjourning to the press room to file their stories. Suddenly the door burst open and Stretton's loyal advisor and assistant Colonel Frank Thorogood called us to order.

'Please,' he said, 'I beg you, do not send the story. They will crucify him in Canberra; you do not understand what this will do to him. He has brought Darwin single-handedly back from the brink. If you send this story it will destroy him. I will do anything … I implore you.' He was close to tears. No one spoke. There was an embarrassing silence until a single voice from the rear carried across the room.

'I have already filed.'

It triggered a mad rush for the phones. Thorogood's shoulders slumped as he left the room.

That evening, Stretton held his usual press conference.

He informed us that he planned to hand over full administrative control to local authorities the next day, with the recommendation that normal civilian administration should resume. Stretton also paid a visit to Government House to discuss the impending visit of the Governor-General, Sir John Kerr, for the official handover. The evacuation had been successful, essential services had been restored to an acceptable level and he felt his mission was almost complete.

## Tuesday 31 December 1974

I was quietly advised Stretton could attempt a low-key exit ahead of the hand-over. We drove out to the airport and there he was. As he was climbing the steps to his aircraft I rushed forward. I wanted to apologise for my part in the courtroom incident. I wanted to tell him of the enormous regard I held for him and to thank him for the friendship and the experience we had both shared. I will always remember his final words.

'Well son, when you study the facts you will find you had as much power here as I did.'

He then turned boarded the C130 aircraft and left. I never saw him again.

## Out of Cyclone Tracy, heroes were born

If one man could be singled out from the many heroes of Darwin it would be General Alan Stretton who in my mind singlehandedly brought an element of normality back to a shell-shocked city. Two days later, after the official handover to the authority our mission too was over.

The year 1974 began with Cyclone Wanda bringing devastating floods to Brisbane and ended in Darwin with a Cyclone called Tracy.

It is said of all those touched by Tracy, 'their lives would never be the same again'.

My life also changed dramatically. From a struggling cadet, my efforts were rewarded by my first grading as a journalist and undoubtedly helped establish a career in media lasting through to my retirement almost 40 years later.

*Excerpts from Mal Walden's memoir 'The Newsman'.*

# A History of Australian Cyclones

A natural disaster is a major adverse event resulting from natural processes of the Earth; examples are floods, hurricanes, tornadoes, volcanic eruptions, earthquakes, tsunamis, and other geologic processes.

## Broome — 1887

One of the first natural disasters recorded in Australia came in the afternoon of 22 April 1887 when a late-seasoned cyclone smashed ashore near the WA pearling settlement of Broome killing 140 people.

The early settlers were caught unaware by the cyclone expecting little more than a strong easterly breeze along its Eighty Mile Beach (Now 90-mile Beach).

This one struck late in the season causing widespread carnage and wiping out most of the settlements pearling schooners and luggers.

## Cape York, Queensland — 1899

The seventh deadliest disaster in Australia is Cyclone Mahina, which is also on record as the deadliest cyclone to occur in Australia.

This cyclone was a Category 5, the strongest of the tropical cyclone categories. Cyclone Mahina hit Bathurst Bay, Cape York on March 4, 1899, wrecking an entire fleet of pearling ships and sinking several schooners. The cyclone caused a 43-foot storm surge at Princess Charlotte Bay that reached around 3 miles inland, destroying everything in its path. It also caused a surge that wiped out a camp at Barrow Point, which is located 40 feet above sea level. Cyclone Mahina continued across the Cape York Peninsula and the Gulf of Carpentaria, lasting for a total of 6 days. Records indicate 283 deaths as a result of this cyclone. However, around 100 indigenous people were also killed and not included in the count because they were not considered part of the population during that time. Final estimates are at 410 deaths.

## Broome — 1910

In 1910 Broome was struck by another destructive cyclone with winds estimated at 175 km/h, killing 40 people, destroying another 20 houses and sinking 34 pearling vessels.

Descriptions of cyclone impacts on the pearling fleet are prominent in the early history of Broome.

In March 1935 a cyclone passed to the north of Broome devastating the pearling fleet at the Lacepede Islands causing the loss of about 141 lives.

## Port Hedland, Broome — 1912

SS Koombana was a passenger and cargo steamship operating along the West Australian coast between Fremantle and ports to the northwest of the state.

On March the 20th 1912, it's believed she struck a tropical cyclone and disappeared along with 74 passengers and 76 crew members. A total of 150 people died.

Her exact location North of Port Hedland has never been confirmed.

Several other ships were also wrecked in the cyclone claiming another 15 lives.

## Mackay — January 1918

The Mackay Cyclone was the first of two cyclones to inflict heavy damage on significant population centres in northern Queensland during early 1918 killing at least 30 people.

Moving in from the Coral Sea late on 20 January with devastating winds which terrified residents as buildings disintegrated, power and water supplies failed, and roofing iron scythed through the air. A storm surge inundated the town around 5:00 am, with large waves reportedly breaking in the centre of Mackay. Phenomenal rainfall over three days generated the worst flooding in Mackay's history causing damage along the coast to Rockhampton where 1,400 homes were flooded.

Railway lines and roads were cut isolating it from the surrounding regions and supplies. It took residents five days to successfully send the word out to signal the alarm and tell the rest of Australia what had happened.

## The Great Gold Coast Cyclone — 1954

The 'Great Gold Coast Cyclone', as it is unofficially known, struck southern Queensland and northern NSW during an era when cyclones went unnamed.

The cyclone caused widespread damage, from Noosa through to Brisbane, the Gold Coast, Byron Bay and Lismore. At least 26 people died during the storm. Byron Bay's entire fishing fleet was swept away and trees measuring more than 1m in diameter were twisted from the ground.

As the eye of the cyclone passed over Macintosh Island on the Gold Coast it brought calmer conditions, which allowed about 30 people to be rescued. Shortly after the rescue, floodwater inundated the island.

## Cyclone Ada — 1970

Ada wreaked havoc on the Whitsunday Island group, off the Queensland coast, over two days on 17 and 18 January 1970. The worst affected were the Daydream, Long, Hook, South Molle and Hayman islands, as well as the area between Bowen and Mackay on the mainland. At least 13 lives were lost during the storm.

## Cyclone Joan — 1975

When Cyclone Joan struck Port Hedland, on the Pilbara coast, it was reported to be one of the strongest ever to have hit the area. About 85 per cent of the houses were damaged, a hospital was destroyed, and dozens of caravans were overturned, which affected the region's many itinerant mine workers. One witness recalled the winds were so strong that small crabs from the sea were blown in under her door. Although there was no loss of human life, graziers suffered heavy losses to livestock.

## Cyclone Alby — 1978

Alby was a rare extra-tropical cyclone that caught residents of southwest WA off guard in April 1978. Very few cyclones reach so far south, but Alby served as a reminder that when they do, they are no less dangerous than their tropical counterparts. Five people died during the cyclone, and it's believed Alby is the most damaging storm ever to have impacted the region. Alby never actually made landfall, but the hot winds that it brought fanned existing bushfires out of control. The fires collectively burnt through roughly 114,000 hectares of forest and farmland.

## Cyclone Winifred — 1986

When Cyclone Winifred crossed the Queensland coast south of Innisfail on 1 February, it was the most disastrous storm that northern Queenslanders had seen in over 14 years claiming at least 3 lives.

A Bureau of Meteorology report on the storm stated that the general public had a relatively poor understanding of tropical cyclones at the time. One elderly man died after being blown from his roof during the storm, one person drowned, and a teenage girl died from injuries caused by flying debris. The damage to crops and infrastructure extended from Cairns to Ingham and was compounded by the flooding of the Herbert and Tully rivers.

## Cyclone Orson — 1989

Though Orson was one of the most powerful cyclones ever to have struck WA, it moved so quickly that many communities were only exposed to its force for a relatively short period.

Orson crossed the coast at Cape Preston, west of Karratha, on 23 April moving at 28 km/h. Wind gusts up to 275 were recorded at a gas rig out to sea shortly before the cyclone made landfall. Several buildings were destroyed in the mining town of Pannawonica, while Karratha and Dampier escaped with minor damage. Four Indonesian fishermen reportedly died in rough seas around Ashmore Island, off the northwest coast of Australia.

## Cyclone Bobby — 1995

Cyclone Bobby travelled the length of the northwest Australian coastline, eventually making landfall near the Pilbara town of Onslow, northeast of Exmouth, just after midnight on 26 February. 8 lives were lost.

More than 400 mm of rain fell around Onslow, and flooding affected many communities throughout western and southern WA. One motorist drowned while attempting to cross a flooded creek, and seven other people died when two fishing trawlers sunk off the coast near Onslow.

## Cyclone Justin — 1997

Cyclone Justin crossed the Queensland coast just north of Cairns on 22 March and moved inland before turning southeast and passing back out to sea. There was widespread damage to the region in and between Cairns and Townsville, caused by a combination of strong winds, heavy rain and storm surges. Two people were killed — one in a landslide near Townsville and another electrocuted by a fallen power line at Innisfail. Earlier in Justin's life, as many as 30 people died in Papua New Guinea.

## Cyclone Ingrid — 2005

Cyclone Ingrid was unusual in that it caused widespread damage in two states and a territory. It crossed Cape York as a category 4; intensified to a category 5 before battering coastal and island communities along the NT's Arnhem Land coast; and crossed WA's Kimberley coast as a category 4. Five people died when large swells capsized their boat near Kerema, in Papua New Guinea.

## Cyclone Larry — 2006

Cyclone Larry struck northern Queensland near Innisfail just a month before Cyclone Monica. The storm and subsequent floods damaged about 10,000 buildings, of which about 500 were destroyed.

Helicopters delivered food and emergency supplies to several townships isolated by the floods. Larry wiped out about 80 per cent of Australia's banana crop, amounting to around $300 million worth of damage. Thousands of people were left without work as a result, and a nationwide banana shortage saw the price of the fruit soar. The cyclone also destroyed about $15 million worth of avocados.

## Cyclone Monica — 2006

Cyclone Monica's powerful wind gusts wiped out a weather station as it neared the Top End coast in April 2006. It moved over fairly remote regions, causing no deaths or serious injuries, although Darwin's ANZAC Day commemorations were cancelled. The Arnhem Land community of Maningrida, 35km from where Monica made landfall, was one of the hardest-hit areas.

## Cyclone George — 2007

When Cyclone George crossed the WA coast northeast of Port Hedland, more than 1,000 people in mining camps were left stranded. Itinerant workers at a camp about 100km southeast of Port Hedland were among the hardest hit. Their temporary accommodations were not built to withstand cyclonic winds and many were destroyed, resulting in two deaths and numerous injuries. George was the most destructive cyclone to affect the Port Hedland region since Cyclone Joan in 1975. Strong winds caused widespread damage, with wind gusts estimated to have reached 200 km/h.

## Cyclone Yasi — 2011

When cyclone Yasi hit Queensland in 2011, it was declared to be one of the most powerful storms the region had seen since records began.

Cyclone Yasi bore down on northern Queensland with all the strength of a category 5 system just days after a category 2 had made landfall 200km to the south. Hospital patients were evacuated from Cairns amid fears the city would suffer a direct hit. But Yasi crossed the coast near Mission Beach, 40km to the south, causing major damage to infrastructure and vegetation around Tully. Yachts in Port Hinchinbrook suffered millions of dollars of damage. One young man was killed — he was asphyxiated by fumes while sheltering inside with his generator.

## Cyclone Marcia — 2015

Cyclone Marcia intensified from a category 2 to a category 5 just before crossing the Queensland coast north of Rockhampton in February 2015.

With wind gusts of almost 300 km/h, it destroyed about 350 homes and damaged almost 2,000 properties in and around Yeppoon and Rockhampton. Pre-empting dangerous coastal erosion, conservation volunteers worked hard to relocate the nests of loggerhead turtles higher up on the beaches near Bundaberg before the cyclone made landfall.

\* \* \* \*

Of all the cyclones in the history of Australia, Cyclone Tracy which struck Darwin on Christmas morning in 1974 remains the most destructive. At least 71 people were killed, and many thousands were injured. Of a population of 43,000, more than half were left homeless.

After covering the impact of the disaster through to the initial reconstruction period I was recalled back to the HSV7 Melbourne Newsroom; besides Cyclone Tracy was no longer the lead story.

A bulk ore carrier had ploughed into the Tasman Bridge in Hobart causing a large section to collapse onto the ship and into the Derwent River below. Twelve people were killed, including seven crewmembers onboard the ship Lake Illawarra.

# Bridges, Mining and Unsung Heroes

**Tasman Bridge, Hobart — 1975**

*'Approaching the crest of the Hobart Bridge ... I could see a bright set of tail lights (ahead) suddenly disappear ... then I spotted the centre white line missing ... the missus is yelling 'stop, stop!' I said 'I don't think I can' ... next thing I know, we were hung over the edge'*
**Survivor Frank Manley**

It was 9:27 pm on the evening of 5th January 1975. Drizzle was falling as light traffic made its way across the giant span of the Hobart Bridge above the Derwent River.

Suddenly the lights went out.

As Frank Manley and his family were approaching the centre of the bridge the white-painted road line suddenly disappeared. His wife began screaming to 'stop', 'stop'. The car slid towards a gap in the bridge coming to a halt with the front wheels hanging precariously over the edge of the broken span.

'The rear wheels had already lost traction from the concrete. Had I put the car in reverse I was convinced the vibration would have sent us over the edge'.

His brother-in-law and daughter, who were in the back seat, were first to escape running frantically back waving their arms to prevent other vehicles from plunging over the edge.

Frank and his wife sat in shock for one brief moment as their HQ GTS Monaro teetered on the brink, see-sawing in the breeze.

Then slowly and gingerly at first, they opened their doors, found their footing on the road, and then leapt clear running in sheer panic back to safety.

Frank Manley recalls the moment he opened the driver's door to make his escape only to see a 45-metre drop to the surging water beneath him. 'It looked like a big black whirlpool ... the water was all stirred up... like a washing machine in a big black hole.'

Holding his seat headrest for support, he stretched his legs until his feet felt the firmness of the road towards the rear of his car.

Almost 50 years later he still believed the only thing that stopped his car from tipping over the edge was the casing of the automatic transmission, which ground and gripped into the surface of the bridge. *"If it was a four-speed (manual), we'd have all died!"*

Alongside his car, a Holden station wagon teetered in the same precarious position, pushed to the edge by another vehicle which had struck them from behind.

This car contained Murray Ling, his wife Helen and two of

their children. He too eased himself and his young family out of the car.

While remarkably the occupants of both vehicles survived, sadly others were not so lucky.

As Murray Ling attempted to flag down other approaching vehicles he stood horrified as two cars ignored his warning, even swerving as they raced past him and hurtled over the edge into the river.

Twelve people were killed, including the occupants of four cars which fell 45 metres after driving off the broken bridge.

As Ling and Manley were leaping to safety with their families, beneath them the ship listed to starboard and sank in 35m of water a short distance to the south.

Seven crew members of the iron ore carrier Lake Illawarra were trapped and drowned. Above that scene, the two cars stayed balanced on the edge of the bridge as if in tribute, until finally removed the following Tuesday.

The subsequent marine court of inquiry found the ship had been off course as it neared the bridge, partly due to the strong tidal current but also because of inattention by the ship's master, Captain Boleslaw Pelc.

On his initial approach to the bridge, Pelc slowed the ship to a 'safe' speed.

Although Lake Illawarra was capable of passing through the bridge's central navigation span, the captain attempted to pass through one of the eastern spans.

Despite several changes, of course, the ship proved unmanageable due to its insufficient speed relative to the current. In desperation, the captain ordered 'full speed astern', at which point, all control was lost.

The vessel drifted towards the bridge crashing into the

pile-capping of piers 18 and 19, bringing three unsupported spans and 127m of roadway crashing onto the vessel's deck. The ship listed to starboard and sank within minutes taking the lives of seven crew members trapped below decks.

The subsequent marine court of inquiry found that the captain had not handled the ship in a proper and seamanlike manner, and his certificate was suspended for six months.

The collapse had a direct and lingering social and economic impact on Hobart. For 30,000 residents on the eastern shore, their 3-minute commute over the bridge turned into a 90-minute nightmare to reach the other side.

Known as 'The Tale of Two Cities' the inconvenience lasted until the Tasman Bridge was re-opened on 8 October 1977, nearly three years after its collapse.

For the families of victims and survivors, the memory of the disaster will last a lifetime — just as those who suffered a similar bridge disaster in Melbourne in 1970.

(Excerpts from multiple media sources and transcripts from the Marine Board of Inquiry)

## West Gate Bridge, Melbourne — 1970

'It began with the sounds of 'pings' and 'pops' as bolts began to blow from sockets, 'like exploding light-bulbs'. Then a soft groaning sound as steal fought a futile effort to maintain its integrity. The Resident Engineer immediately phoned for advice. His last words were "Shall I get the bods off?" (referring to the workers). At that moment the 'world fell from under their feet'.

Official records, evidence and transcripts from a Royal Commission.

It was 11:50 on the morning of 15th October 1970 and just two years into the construction of Melbourne's Westgate steal box-girder Bridge.

Workers were milling around, chatting during a lunch break in huts directly beneath the Bridge.

Above them, welders, riggers and supervisors were suddenly aware of a slight movement and strange sounds. Then silence.

The span of the bridge in question was 128 metres of concrete and steel which began to gently tremble, gathering momentum as if 'suffering a terminal convulsion'. Suddenly the steel changed colour under stress. Seconds later it exploded.

Then, in the blink of an eye, span 10-11 of the construction phase, weighing 2000 tons broke away and dropped 50 metres onto the worker's sheds below crushing them into the mud and depths of the Yarra River.

The two spans were being brought together but as they became close it was obvious they wouldn't quite meet.

There was a gap of approximately 10cm. So, to straighten that gap, weights were applied which created a buckle. Instructions were given to straighten the buckle "without further delay".

Starting at around 8:30 that fateful morning the task of straightening the buckle began with the removal of a large number of bolts.

Around 11:00 am, Jack Hindshaw, the Resident Engineer was advised things were not going well. He arrived on-site and was instantly aware that a potentially dangerous situation was imminent and immediately phoned for advice.

At that moment, the world fell from under their feet.

Thirty-five construction workers were killed and 18 injured, remaining Australia's worst industrial accident to this day.

TV cameramen Reg Boulter from HSV7 and Ray Rowe from GTV9 were first on the scene. They had been sitting in the press room at police headquarters in the city monitoring the official police radio when it suddenly 'went dead, went quiet.' It was a signal something big was about to break.

Both men rushed to their news cars in time to overhear a police announcement on their radio receiver. 'It's definitely collapsed. The bridge has collapsed.'

At that same time, phone calls were being received in all media newsrooms.

The noise of the impact had been heard 20 kilometres away and buildings hundreds of metres from the disaster were shaken and sprayed with mud.

Ambulances and emergency workers rushed to the site from all over the city as volunteers and survivors frantically dug for buried and trapped mates; many with injuries themselves had to be restrained. Bedlam and frustration led to clashes with Boulter and Rowe who stood among them. 'The footage we filmed was just incredible. Bodies hanging from girders. Survivors calling for help'. Images Boulter says that would live with him forever.

In a bid to get their vision back to their respective channels, they called a colleague from a motorcycle gang who collected their film canisters, delivering those first images to both HSV7 and GTV9. Meanwhile, networks arrived to set up micro links close to the scene where they began their 24-hour cycle of live news crosses.

According to Archives held by Public Record Office Victoria.

"Rescuers worked all afternoon and far into the night, always in horrifying conditions, often in peril of death or injury themselves.

A fire broke out as a result of spilt diesel oil igniting; while quickly extinguished, the fire added to the difficulties of rescue work...

All that was humanly possible to save lives and mitigate the suffering of the injured was undoubtedly done".

Amid the nationwide grief and horror, Premier Sir Henry Bolte announced the establishment of a Royal Commission to investigate the cause of the collapse.

The report, tabled in parliament in 1971, detailed several factors that contributed to the bridge's failure and left no party associated with the collapse blameless.

It concluded: "The disaster which occurred... and the tragedy of the 35 deaths was utterly unnecessary. That it should have been allowed to happen was inexcusable. The reasons for the collapse are to be found in the acts and omissions of those entrusted with building a bridge of a new and highly sophisticated design. Among those engaged in the design and construction of the steel spans, there were mistakes, miscalculations, errors of judgement, failure of communication and inefficiency. To greater or less degree, the Authority itself, the designers, the contractors, even the labour engaged in the work, must all take some part of the blame."

## From Disasters Heroes are Born

Through a tight police cordon, the rescuers came. A constant stream of ambulances, nurses, doctors, priests, Salvation army workers, and even Boy Scouts assisted where they could. But none were as brave as those who had been injured and despite attempts to restrain them, they kept digging for lost mates.

John Laino, who had been digging since he survived the collapse, helped identify the dead and the unconscious.

Bill Snowden of Geelong escaped just in time but returned to dig out a mate and sat with him until the ambulances came.

John Doody, 20, the long-haired larrikin' from Ascot Vale, refused to stop when the rescuers moved in. He carried the injured and dead and dug in the mud for the missing until he collapsed with exhaustion. Ambulance men brought him around and ordered him to go home. He returned within the hour.

The West Gate Bridge collapse on 15 October 1970 became the catalyst for landmark reforms in Victorian workplace health and safety practices.

Excerpts from Bill Hitchins, multimedia coverage and testimony from the subsequent Royal Commission.

# Mining Disasters

'It's been described as 'Australia's Chernobyl'.

> *If the death toll reaches 50,000 (and many believe that is a conservative estimate) the history of Wittenoom will represent not only the greatest mining disaster but perhaps the greatest disaster in Australia's history*
> Asbestos Disease Society of Australia.

## Wittenoom disaster 1943 — 1966

Wittenoom, more than one thousand kilometres northeast of Perth, was once the Pilbara region's largest town and a monument of prosperity.

Today its legacy lies in its blue dust and scorched earth; serving a life sentence in isolation following the deaths of at least 2,000 locals and indirectly more than 42,000 Australians (2022).

Between 700 and 800 Australians are diagnosed with asbestos-related illnesses each year and there is no known cure.

In April 1943 Colonial Sugar Company (CSR) through its subsidiary, Australian Blue Asbestos Ltd took over both the Wittenoom and Vampire Mines and the operation boomed. Exposure to dust was an accepted part of the mining industry, so even the abnormally bad conditions at Wittenoom were accepted by managers and many workers. However, three years later the first health risks were raised. Those risks were mainly ignored and the mining continued.

In 1957 an agreement was reached with James Hardie on the purchase of Wittenoom's blue asbestos for use in Hardie's asbestos-cement building materials.

After the purchase, James Hardie Industries Ltd moved to the Netherlands (then to Ireland) in what has since been claimed as an attempt to divorce itself from a mounting asbestos crisis.

Before the mine shut down in 1966 — due to declining profitability — the town population and former workers were reporting serious illnesses.

Tragically 2,000 of those residents were the first to die and the contagion from blue asbestos was quickly spreading far beyond Wittenoom.

In 1988 a Supreme Court jury found that CSR had been "recklessly indifferent" to the safety of its workers and knowingly allowed the processing of asbestos to continue even though the dangers of asbestos fibre inhalation were known as early as 1926.

From the obvious construction industry, automotive and commercial industries to everyday home appliances. From filters in early-model hair dryers to gaskets and sealers in plumbing and electrical industries.

Printing facilities particularly newspaper offices posed a high risk of asbestos exposure. Printing machines with gaskets and rollers, particularly in Linotype insulation, utilized an extremely high amount of asbestos materials.

While most of us become exposed to asbestos fibres throughout our lives only the unfortunate become victims.

Many then seek legal advice and if it's found to be a workplace illness victims tend to slip under a veil of silence, tied to compensation payments and confidentiality clauses.

An exception to that rule was a former media colleague and one of Melbourne's most experienced sports journalists Trevor Grant. After privately confirming his shocking diagnosis to family, friends and associates, he then went public.

## Trevor Grant

'... I had the terminal disease that twists tongues as well as lungs: mesothelioma... simply impossible, I thought.

As a journalist who'd worked for 40 years for Melbourne's two main newspaper companies, The Age and the Herald and Weekly Times, I just didn't fit the bill. There must be some mistake... To me, mesothelioma victims were easily defined.

They were the poor souls who'd spent their lives working in close contact with the fine dust of asbestos or even the wives who'd washed out their husbands' asbestos-covered overalls at the end of the day. They were plumbers or electricians or builders, not journalists.

It was only after contacting the legal firm Slater and Gordon that I discovered the insidious tentacles of this disease have spread far and wide through the community, to a point where it is no longer correct to describe it as rare. My oncologist tells me he gets a new patient every month who was much the same as me — totally disbelieving they had the disease.

What I discovered through the process of a Supreme Court action I launched in September last year (2015) shocked me to the core. I discovered I had been working close to the dangers of asbestos for decades, both at The Age building at 250 Spencer Street, where I worked from 1969-1970 and 1978-1989, and the Herald office on 44-74 Flinders Street, where I worked from 1970-74 and 1989-1996.

Records showed workers in both these buildings, mostly printers and tradesmen working with insulation, had contracted mesothelioma during these times. I worked on separate floors from these people, but I'd had a lot of regular contact with many on the printing and composing room floors, especially as a young sub-editor.

... mesothelioma can lay dormant in your body for decades. Then, when it suddenly begins to grow, there are few warning signs. This is why it's such devastating cancer. You have little idea it's there until it's grown big enough to cause pain, as in my case, by pushing against the nerves of the chest wall.

The Age and Herald and Weekly Times, along with the infamous makers of asbestos-riddled products, James Hardie, agreed to settle my case out of court, which included a significant payout to me.

In legal terms, this is not an admission of guilt by any of them. At the same time, I know I'm not responsible for my terminal illness.

I expected to be angry about all this; angry about a cynical corporation (Hardie) risking so many thousands of lives, including my own, for the sake of its bottom line; angry every time I saw the foreign minister Julie Bishop on television and was reminded she was paid handsomely as a lawyer to represent one of these vulture corporations; angry that nobody warns potential victims that they had worked in places where others had contracted the disease...

... but all I feel is sadness; sadness not just that I'm going to die prematurely, but sadness that I live in a society that, so often and so easily, still writes off human lives as collateral damage in the pursuit of profit.

Financial compensation is now available to many mesothelioma victims, but only because of the courage and persistence of working-class campaigners such as the late Bernie Banton*.

*Above all else, I want to die happy.*
*(Extracts from The Drum/Trevor Grant, Sports journalist, Melbourne)*

Trevor Grant died on 5 March 2017.

By 2022 the total death toll in Australia was estimated to have reached 45,200. A further 700 to 800 Australians are diagnosed with asbestos-related illnesses each year.

There are alarming fears that once the dust has finally settled the death toll from Wittenoom could reach 60,000 by 2030 becoming the greatest occupational health and safety tragedy in the history of Australia — comparable to the Chernobyl nuclear disaster and India's Bhopal gas catastrophe.

Today the town stands as a stark reminder of the dangers of choosing progress over safety, and of the many unheeded warnings. Like Chernobyl; Wittenoom is still one of the most contaminated sites in the world.

*Bernard Banton AM was an Australian social justice campaigner, who became the widely recognized face leading the legal and political fight for compensation for the many sufferers of asbestos-related conditions linked to James Hardie Company and products. On 17 August 2007, he was also diagnosed with terminal peritoneal mesothelioma asbestos cancer, dying a short 103 days later.

> *'Despite offering better respite for patients and earlier detection of disease, we still have no definitive treatment or cure'*
> — *Asbestos Diseases Society of Australia.*

The history of the Australian mining industry began, very modestly; almost 'by chance'.

The first discovery of coal was made by escaped convicts near Newcastle in 1791 just three years after the First Fleet arrived. This was the beginning of Australia's coal industry, now one of the largest coal exporters in the world.

In the 1850s the gold rush placed our mining industry on the world map.

Tin was discovered in 1871 in Tasmania, and then in Inverell in NSW. Soon, Australia's great mines were established — silver, lead and zinc at Broken Hill in NSW.

The Pilbara iron ore region was developed in WA, and new metals were discovered in the second part of the 20th century including bauxite, nickel, tungsten, uranium, oil and natural gas. But mining came at a huge human cost that continues to resonate to this day.

## Old Bulli Colliery — 1887

On March 23, 1887, an explosion in the Hill End section of the Old Bulli Colliery caused the deaths of 81 men and boys.

The subsequent investigation found the explosion was caused by a build-up of methane being ignited by a miner's uncovered lantern.

The investigating commission was scathing in its findings and placed the blame firmly on mine management and the miners themselves, citing their lackadaisical approach to safety as the predominant cause of the explosion.

If indeed that was the cause then it's almost inconceivable to believe lessons were never learnt.

## Mt Kembla 1902

In 1902 at 2 pm on the afternoon of July 31, the Mt Kembla Colliery exploded, killing 96 men and boys.

This blast, which was heard in nearby Wollongong, had an enormous impact on the Illawarra region and more specifically on the village of Mt Kembla, where the shattering effect of lives lost and families torn apart resonates to this day.

It is now a known fact that gas was present in the Mt Kembla coal mine, yet miners strapped on their helmets with a naked flame and a huge blast occurred similar to the blast at the Bulli mine 15 years earlier.

Controversy surrounded the cause. Mine management disputed that gasses were the cause of the Kembla blast claiming their mine to be "one of the best-ventilated mines in the State".

Rather than holding any individual official responsible, the inquiry stated that only the substitution of safety lamps for flame lights could have saved the lives of the 96 victims. However, flame lights continued to be used well into the 1940s.

The Bulli and Mt Kembla colliery disasters claimed 177 lives, and to this day remain two of the largest man-made disasters outside of war.

## Chronology of other mining disasters

1898    a massive methane explosion destroyed the Dudley Colliery in Newcastle killing 14 men.

1908    Mount Morgan September 6, seven miners were entombed under 3,000 tons of rock during a collapse in the town's gold mine.

1912    Fire in the Mount Lyell Mine became an epic disaster killing 42 who were left trapped due to no emergency warning system operating in the mine.

1921    a coal dust explosion in the brand-new Mount Mulligan Mine caused the deaths of at least 75 workers. It took five months from the time of the accident to recover the bodies of all victims.

1923    the Bellbird Colliery near Maitland in NSW claimed 21 lives.

1929    a dam burst at the Briseis Tin Mine in Tasmania claiming 14 lives including a family of five who was sitting down to a meal when their home was swept away.

1954    in another massive blow to the Queensland coal industry a huge gas blast at the Collinsville mine — later said to have been almost pure carbon dioxide — left seven men dead from asphyxiation.

| | |
|---|---|
| 1972 | was yet another disaster for the Queensland coal industry when a huge gas blast ripped through The Box Flat Mine just outside Ipswich killing 17 men. |
| 1975 | a huge explosion ripped through central Queensland's Kianga No. 1 mine killing 13 men. Their bodies were never recovered after a decision to seal the mine. |
| 1986 | a huge blast occurred in the Moura number 1 coal mine 200 kilometres SW of Rockhampton killing 12. Another 8 miraculously survived. |
| 1994 | tragedy struck again this time at the Moura number 2 mine when an explosion trapped 11 workers. Unfortunately, another explosion occurred during a rescue attempt forcing the mine to be sealed as a permanent tomb. |
| 1996 | the Gretley mine disaster near Newcastle claimed the lives of four men swept away and drowned following a sudden inrush of water.<br><br>It was later found that a machine had dug into old workings of a nearby disused Colliery, from where the water came. |
| 1999 | disaster struck at Northparkes Mines in central NSW when four workers were killed instantly under millions of tonnes of earth and rocks in a collapse caused by a catastrophic air blast 140 metres below the ground. |

## 2006 Beaconsfield, Tasmania

At 9:26 on the morning of 25 April 2006, a small earthquake triggered an underground rockfall at the Beaconsfield gold mine in northern Tasmania.

Of the seventeen people who were in the mine at the time, fourteen escaped the collapse of one of its main shafts. However, the seismic event measuring just 2.3 on the Richter scale brought down tonnes of rock which killed miner Larry Knight (44) and trapped his two colleagues Todd Russell (34) and Brant Webb (37) — almost one kilometre below the surface.

Knight was killed in the initial rockfall, but Webb and Russell were trapped alive in a part of the vehicle in which they had been working at the time. Webb had been knocked unconscious and Russell's lower body was completely buried. When both sufficiently recovered they began working together to free themselves. They survived by drinking groundwater that dripped through the rocks and sharing half a muesli bar. Then they lay in the rubble for the next 14 days.

Above them, the biggest rescue operation in Australia's history had been mobilised attracting a massive local and international media audience beaming the story around the world.

Unaware that two miners had survived, rescuers tunnelled and dug in dangerous conditions until they reached the body of Larry Knight on 27 April.

It wasn't until 30 April two rescuers, Pat Ball (the underground manager) and Steve Saltmarsh (the mine foreman) entered the collapsed level and called out. Once they heard Webb and Russell respond, they immediately confirmed both men were still alive.

On 8 May after a series of delicate drilling operations, rescuers Glenn Burns, Donovan Lightfoot and Royce Gill finally reached the trapped miners.

Brant Webb was freed at 4:47 am followed by Todd Russell seven minutes later. At two minutes to 6 am on May 9, both men walked out of the lift cage, punching their fists in the air to the cheers of the Beaconsfield crowds who had gathered outside the mine gate.

There were many heroes from a team of more than 280; eleven of whom received official awards for bravery. However, as in previous mining tragedies, many unsung heroes stepped up with selfless acts of bravery and a community whose efforts helped unite a township facing tragedy.

Russell and Webb's ordeal has since become folklore. The pair signed media contracts and rose to celebrity status before they were immortalised in the 2012 telemovie Beaconsfield. Respected journalist Richard Carleton is also remembered after he died of a heart attack at the scene.

In 2011 a museum at the site became a major tourist attraction for the town of Beaconsfield and a tribute to Larry Knight who died on that tragic Anzac Day in 2006.

Today the mining industry boasts significant improvements in health and safety over the last decade, reducing the incidence of both fatalities and serious injuries. However, it still has one of the highest rates of fatalities in any industry in Australia.

For that reason alone, we need the heroes and the selfless acts of bravery that we have witnessed so many times in the past.

'The legacy of heroes is the memory they create and the inheritance of their great example.'

Adapted from the words of Benjamin Disraeli. Ian Jamieson former president of the Tasmanian Mining Industry Union Council

# Quakes, Quivers and Miraculous Escapes

'We thought it was the spirit of our gods rising up to speak with us... then we saw the spirit had made all the kangaroos fall down on the ground... so we took those kangaroos and we ate them and people were sick...white powder killed a lot of kangaroos [and] spinifex [grass]. Water was on fire, that's what we saw... and then the spirit left'.

Nyarri Morgan was an Aboriginal survivor from Maralinga
— ABC.

Earthquakes in Australia are unpredictable and infrequent, but when they strike they cause massive disruption. Meckering in the West to Newcastle in the East are prime examples. A fatal landslide struck the NSW ski-resort town of Thredbo but nowhere did the earth move more than Maralinga in S.A. during nuclear testing; a disastrous chapter in Australian history.

## Maralinga Nuclear Tests

On September 27, 1956, at the desolate site of Maralinga — part of the Woomera Prohibited Area about 800 kilometres northwest of Adelaide — the countdown began.

Military personnel, scientists, technicians and officers positioned close to the blast zone — tensed themselves in readiness to report on the effects of the first Maralinga atomic bomb test.

As the count reached its finale – three... two... one... FLASH! - all present were ordered to turn their backs.

Those who placed their hands across their eyes reported seeing the bones of their fingers through their hands, like an x-ray, such as the brightness of the flash.

When given the order to turn back again they saw an awesome rising fireball before the mushroom cloud began to bloom and blow across the desert.

October the following year, there will have been six more tests.

The United Kingdom conducted 12 major nuclear weapons tests in Australia between 1952 and 1957 involving approximately 16,000 Australian civilians who were exposed to the nuclear fallout.

Three at the Montebello Islands

Two at Emu fields

Seven at Maralinga

Seven of the bombs tested at Maralinga alone were double the force of the bomb dropped on the Japanese city of Hiroshima in World War 2. Many minor tests were conducted under strict secrecy.

Subsequent inquiries found many Australian servicemen were ordered to repeatedly fly through the mushroom clouds from atomic explosions, without protection; and to march into ground zero immediately after bomb detonation.

Local indigenous groups around Maralinga spoke about a black mist of radioactive dust sweeping over their communities following the explosions.

Documents would later reveal hundreds of children and grandchildren of veterans exposed to radiation were born with shocking illnesses including tumours, down syndrome, cleft palates, cerebral palsy, autism, missing bones and heart disease.

But the link between exposure to radiation at the test sites and subsequent illness of the veterans and their descendants has never been accepted by the Australian Government.

It's a stark contrast to a British study in 1999, which found that 30 per cent of their test veterans had died, mostly in their 50s, from cancers or cancer-related illnesses.

An initial clean-up of the contaminated radioactive site was attempted in 1967. However, in 1985 a Royal Commission into the effects of the tests found that significant radiation hazards still existed in many of the Maralinga test areas.

It recommended another clean-up, which was completed in 2000 for $108 million.

The debate has continued over the safety of the site and the long-term health effects on the traditional Aboriginal custodians and former personnel.

In 2017, the Australian government expanded medical benefits for members of the nuclear testing program, but most are now in their late 80s and one told the ABC the move was "too bloody late".

Today observers report that if you look closely, you can still see the ground is covered with what looks like broken glass, where the soil was so intensely hot from the blasts it melted and turned to silicon.

And even after all this time, the natural vegetation still hasn't sufficiently grown back. Locals say even animals and birds in the area have not returned.

More than half a century on they describe the day their earth moved at Maralinga as a disastrous chapter in Australian history

# Trains, Planes and a Black Box of Tricks

'A violent jolt was the first indication then my world was tipped on its axis... followed by sounds of screeching metal, breaking glass, splintered wood and screaming... a sensation of flying and blackness... then excruciating pain'.
Granville survivors.

### Granville — 1977

Tuesday 18th of January 1977 has been seared into the psyche of the western Sydney suburb of Granville — synonymous today with the worst train disaster in Australia's history.

The events began at 6:09 that morning when the regular weekday commuter departed on time from Mt Victoria in the Blue Mountains bound for Sydney carrying 469 passengers.

Two minutes after departing Parramatta and three minutes behind schedule it entered a curve travelling at the maximum permitted speed of 80km/h on its approach to Granville station.

Suddenly without warning the locomotive engine derailed which caused carriages 1 and 2 to come off the tracks behind it.

The engine then proceeded uncontrolled for another 46 metres before striking and demolishing one of the steel trestles supporting the Bold Street Bridge coming to rest on one side some distance beyond.

The first carriage, which had broken free, was torn open when it collided with a severed mast beside the track, killing eight passengers.

Carriage 2 which had become detached came to rest against a retaining wall largely intact.

The rear half of the third carriage, and the forward half of the fourth carriage, came to rest under the weakened bridge, whose weight was estimated at 570 tonnes.

Within seconds, with all its supports demolished, the bridge with several cars on top of it collapsed onto the wooden framed carriages, crushing the passengers in their seats below. Some areas were crushed to floor level.

Out of disaster heroes are born and within seconds several surviving passengers were first to assist the injured, applying tourniquets, offering comforting words to the injured and soothing words to the dying.

Then came the cavalry, a vast rescue mission of the police, firefighters, ambulance crews, doctors, nurses, engineers and railway workers among them.

Immediate attempts were made to raise the bridge to provide safer access for rescuers. Then doctors, nurses and police were able to crawl into tiny spaces to reach the injured.

In one instance, a police officer crawled through a 35cm gap between victims' bodies to reach an injured man.

A doctor had to amputate the arm of a dead woman to give the rescuer access but then without warning, a slab of concrete slipped another 5cm, injuring the officer's back.

Rescuers were also hindered by leaking LPG gas from the train's heating system which threatened the immediate use of power tools.

The accident also drew civilian volunteers, some just teenagers, to lend a hand but very soon a crowd of ghoulish sightseers also turned up. By 8:50 am, 1,500 people had lined the cutting, many spilling onto tracks hindering the rescue attempts before police were forced to move in.

The last living person was freed around 6 pm but died in the hospital. The last body was extracted 31 hours after the crash.

In all, 84 people died including an unborn baby who was added to the toll in 2017. More than 210 were injured.

An inquiry headed by NSW District Court Chief Judge, Justice James Staunton, began in February 1977.

It found failures reaching into the highest echelons of the Public Transport Commission exacerbated by a high turnover of track inspection staff in the months before the disaster. The track was in a "very unsatisfactory condition", poorly fastened and badly aligned.

Although no one was held directly accountable, among his recommendations, Justice Staunton called for senior emergency personnel to be trained in disaster management and a provision for more general training for health and welfare workers in traumatic events.

It also revealed that the Bold Street bridge had been struck by derailments on the same section of track twice before — by a locomotive in 1967 and a loaded coal wagon in 1975.

Each year since the Granville disaster, survivors, rescuers and loved ones of those killed gather on the Bold Street bridge on January 18 for a memorial service, dropping roses to remember those lost.

Today the name Granville is synonymous with the worst rail accident in Australia's history. However, since the first commuter train ran between Melbourne's Flinders Street Station and the Port of Melbourne in 1854, hundreds have died in a frightening chronology of Australian train crashes.

April 20, 1908, Sunshine (near Melbourne)
Two trains collided in the station killing 44 people.

July 18, 1910, Richmond, Victoria
9 people were killed when their train hit a locomotive in fog.

March 16, 1914, Exeter, NSW
14 people died when 2 trains collided in fog.

June 9, 1925, Traveston, Queensland
10 people were killed when a train derailed on a bridge.

September 13, 1926, Murulla, NSW
A Sydney-bound passenger train collided with runaway goods wagons killing 27 people.

June 10, 1926, Aberdeen, NSW
A Sydney-Brisbane express fell from a timber bridge. Five people died, and 50 were injured.

May 8, 1943, Wodonga, Victoria
25 servicemen and women were killed when a train collided with their bus on a level crossing.

Jan 20, 1944, Brooklyn, NSW
17 died when a mail train collided with a bus on a level crossing.

May 5, 1947, Camp Mountain, Queensland
A train derailment killed 16 people.

October 18, 1947, Tamaree, Queensland
8 people were killed when mail trains collided.

February 24, 1951, Horsham, Victoria
11 died when a train collided with a bus on a level crossing.

May 7, 1952, Berala, Sydney
A rail accident killed 10 and injured 81.

June 1, 1952, Boronia, Victoria
9 died when a train collided with a bus on a level crossing.

December 19, 1953, Sydenham, Sydney
5 people died and 748 were injured when two passenger trains collided.

February 26, 1960, Bogantungan, Queensland
7 people died when a bridge collapsed as the Rockhampton-bound "Midlander" passed over it. The bridge had been weakened by floodwater.

February 7, 1969, Violet Town, Victoria
The Violet Town rail accident is also known as the southern Aurora disaster. Sydney-Melbourne Express, travelling at 120 km/h was involved in a collision with a goods train leaving 9 dead and 117 injured.

January 18, 1977, Granville, Sydney
Australia's worst-ever railway disaster. 83 were killed when a commuter train derailed and crashed into the pillars of a bridge bringing it down on top of the train.

May 6, 1990, Cowan
6 people died north of Sydney when an Intercity express train crashed into a vintage steam train.

December 2, 1999, Glenbrook (Blue Mountains)
7 died, and 51 were injured when a Lithgow commuter train slammed into the rear of the Indian Pacific.

October 24, 2002, Adelaide
4 people died when the Ghan interstate train and a bus carrying schoolchildren collided at a level crossing.

June 5th 2007, Kerang train disaster
11 died and 23 were injured when a train and truck collided at a crossing near Kerang in Victoria making this the deadliest Australian rail disaster since 1977.

February 20, 2020, Wallan, Victoria
2 were killed (the driver and co-driver) when the Sydney to

Melbourne XPT carrying more than 150 passengers derailed north of Melbourne.

* * * *

While risks are associated with all forms of transport major 'air' disasters are relatively rare in Australia today, but the history of aviation has left a tragic legacy in its wake.

# Australian Aviation Disasters

### TAA's ill-fated Fokker Friendship 1960

Pilot. 'Roger tower will commence let down to approach on runway 32'.

Control tower. 'Cleared for visual approach wind (calm) report final approach, confirm...'

Nothing more was heard from TAA flight 538.

June 10, 1960, TAA flight 538 was completing a scheduled flight from Brisbane to Mackay. The aircraft was Australia's first Fokker Friendship outside Europe, obtained by TAA and named Abel Tasman after the Dutch explorer.

It left Brisbane at 5 pm stopping at Townsville to refuel and take on another 7 adults and nine schoolboys adding to the nine passengers already on board.

All the schoolboys were boarders at Rockhampton Grammar returning home to Mackay for the Queen's birthday long weekend.

Experienced pilot captain F C Pollard then took off bound for Mackay.

At 8:17 pm Mackay air traffic controller, E W Miskell reported that fog had rolled in temporarily closing the airport at which Pollard informed the tower that he would place his aircraft in a holding position at 13,000 feet pending clearance.

At 8:40 pm conditions improved and Flight 538 was advised to make its landing. As the aircraft approached close to the runway threshold, at a height of about 50 feet, the pilot advised that a small patch of fog had suddenly appeared on the runway. It then flew along the runway at a height of approximately 50 ft before aborting the landing and commenced to climb away.

Two approaches were made and subsequently aborted.

By 10 pm the fog had lifted and conditions were described as a 'bright moonlit night with a completely calm sea' and the tower advised Pollard to approach runway 32.

Pollard acknowledged the transmission 'Roger tower, will commence let down to approach on runway 32'. That was the final word from flight 538.

Miskell transmitted 'Confirm again' until 10:05 pm when

he alerted emergency services and a full-scale search and rescue operation was launched.

Five hours later at 3 am Saturday 11 June a searching boat located the wreckage, including damaged passenger seats, clothing and cabin furnishings, floating five nautical miles east of Mackay.

All 29 people on board Trans Australia Airlines Flight 538 were killed.

A board of inquiry was launched in July of that year but could not determine a particular cause. One possibility was an altimeter malfunction. Another possibility was a misinterpretation of the equipment. The most significant recommendation was the introduction of flight box flight recorders to be installed in all passenger-carrying aircraft of that size or larger.

If heroes are born out of disasters then recognition should go to Dr David Warren the Australian inventor of the world's first black box flight recorder in 1953. (* see tribute following)

There is a certain irony Australia's worst aviation accident also occurred in Mackay but was surrounded by wartime secrecy.

## Mackay 1943

At 6:00 am on a foggy morning on the 14th of June 1943, a United States B-17C took off from Mackay Airport bound for Port Moresby, New Guinea.

Onboard it carried 6 crew and 35 passengers, all US servicemen. There was only seating for the crew so the passengers were required to sit on the floor straddling the person in front with no seat belts.

The plane climbed through a fog layer and levelled out at about 300 feet before commencing a left turn.

Then suddenly, it plunged into bushland at Bakers Creek,

a small community about 8 km south of the airport. A fireball erupted killing 40 of the 41 occupants and leaving just one survivor.

Due to wartime censorship, the incident was hushed up. Nothing could be reported until August 1945, when details of the crash slowly began to unfold.

It was and remains today, Australia's worst aviation disaster.

## Melbourne 1938

One of the worst early civil aviation disasters involved the Kyeema, a National Australian Airlines passenger plane carrying 18 passengers and crew. The Douglas DC-2 had left Adelaide on the morning of October 25, its passengers including a federal parliamentarian, Charles Hawker, three high-profile South Australian winemakers — Hugo Grant, Tom Hardy and Sidney Hill Smith — a honeymoon couple and several barristers.

It's feared the flight crew mistook the town of Sunbury from the air for Daylesford, putting them 30 kilometres off course. Believing they were on the final approach to Essendon airport, in heavy cloud, they slammed into the western slopes of Mount Dandenong killing all on board.

A subsequent royal commission saw new regulations requiring flight-checking officers to monitor flights, weather and alternative landing options.

## Perth 1950

On 26 June 1950 a Douglas DC-4 Skymaster, 'Amana', the flagship of Australian National Airways, took off from Guildford

(Perth) for a flight to Melbourne via Adelaide. As the aircraft flew eastwards over the outer suburbs of Perth numerous witnesses observed that it was flying at a lower altitude than usual for the daily Skymaster services. At least one of the engines was running roughly and backfiring at regular intervals. In the minutes before it crashed, witnesses heard several different engine sounds including what was described as a very loud, high-pitched "scream".

The crew turned left in an attempt to return to the airport. In a 15-degree turn, the aircraft barely cleared a ridgeline, struck a tree 30 feet off the ground and ploughed into a downward slope.

All 29 occupants were killed in the accident; one initially survived but died six days later.

An inquiry could not determine the cause of this disaster, either, though some investigators suspected water in the fuel tank. It was Australia's worst aviation accident at the time.

## Longreach — 1966

The 1960s were to prove the worst decade for the Australian airline industry.

On September 22, 1966, an Ansett ANA Vickers Viscount passenger plane flying from Mount Isa to Longreach burst into flame above central Queensland, about 20 kilometres west of Winton. The fire began in a cabin blower, spread to a fuel tank and melted a spar supporting the left wing.

The wing fell off and the plane crashed, killing all 24 passengers and crew.

## Port Hedland 1968

Two years later, in December 1968, another Vickers Viscount, this one operated by MacRobertson-Miller Airlines, lost its right wing in flight near Port Hedland, Western Australia.

The plane was flying from Perth to Port Hedland when more than half the wing and an engine separated from the craft, which crashed about 50 kilometres from its destination. All 26 passengers and crew perished, making it the third-worst civil aviation disaster in Australian history.

Unexplained maintenance problems were blamed. No single air crash has killed so many people in Australia since, though multiple deaths have continued to be recorded.

## Lockhart River — 2005

The greatest number of deaths in a single crash since the 1968 disaster at Port Hedland occurred on May 7, 2005, when 15 people died after a Fairchild Metroliner crashed near Lockhart River in far-north Queensland.

An inquiry found pilot error was to blame. The plane, owned by Transair Ltd and operated by Aerotopics, was approaching to land at Lockhart River Airport when it struck a ridge known as South Pap and crashed, killing all aboard.

In summary, accidents involving air transport are incredibly rare. Flying in pure jet-powered aircraft has a perfect fatality-free safety record in Australia. Other types of flying machines do carry some risks. For example, 40 fatalities were recorded in the aviation sector in 2017, a significant increase from the 21 fatalities in 2016 and a further rise in 2019.

But once again the Australian carrier Qantas has maintained its status as the number one airline over all others. Australia's Airline safety has also been attributed to another great hero Dr David Warren.

## The Black Box

In 1954 the Melbourne-based Aeronautical Research Laboratory (ARL) at Fishermen's Bend was asked to help investigate a series of crashes involving the world's first Comet jetliners.

As the senior research scientist, David Warren took more than just a passing interest in the Comet crashes. His father died in a 1934 plane crash in Bass Strait and it had often occurred to him how extremely useful it would have been to have recorded the events immediately before the crash.

As he proceeded to analyse details of the comet crashes he suddenly visualised the world's first miniature wire recorder he had seen at a recent trade show. It was an instrument that recorded music, but it immediately occurred to him that if a similar recorder was carried in the cockpit of an aircraft there could be a record of everything that was said up until the very moment of a crash.

"What if the pilots themselves could tell us what was happening?"

Warren would later concede it was obvious that a tape recording would not survive a burning plane crash, but a wire voice recorder was an option that became the basis for his first 'black box'. Working with instrument colleagues at ARL they found a way of putting flight data and voice recordings onto the wire. This led to the construction of a much-improved version in the late 1950s.

It was only after the crash of a Fokker Friendship in Queensland in 1960 that the inquiry judge strongly recommended black box flight recorders be installed in all airliners and from that moment Australia became the first country in the world to make the cockpit voice recorder mandatory.

In 2016, Dr David Warren was posthumously recognised with the most prestigious aviation award in the industry for his outstanding contribution to transport safety. His pioneering efforts not only significantly improved aviation safety and saved countless lives but the concept of flight recorders is now being utilised in other transport modes such as road, rail and shipping. David Warren passed away in 2010 at the age of 85 and was buried in a casket bearing the inscription: "Flight Recorder Inventor; Do Not Open."

(Australian Transport Safety Bureau and extract from *Icons and Legends*, Brolga Publishing)

# War time Heroes

'.. *the wharf was still burning... the whole scene was one of devastation...bodies washed up on beaches... men collecting the dead ... so many ships smouldering... I waited with four sisters who had volunteered to help'.*
*Matron Edith McQuade White — Darwin 1942.*

On 3 September 1939, Prime Minister Robert Gordon Menzies announced the beginning of Australia's involvement in the World War 2.

Total battle casualties would exceed 72,800.

While Australian civilians did not suffer as other populations did during World War 2 when our homeland was directly threatened the impact was just as painful.

## Darwin — 1942

On 19th February 1942, mainland Australia came under attack for the first time in its history when Japanese forces launched two air raids on Darwin.

They were the first of 97 attacks in various forms; from large-scale raids by medium bombers, torpedo attacks on ships and strafing runs by fighters.

In the first and deadliest attack, 242 aircraft hit the town of Darwin, local airfields and ships in the harbour.

The first attack ceased after approximately 40 minutes. The second attack, which began an hour later, involved a high-altitude bombing which lasted for 20-25 minutes.

The two raids killed at least 243 people and left between 300-400 wounded.

Twenty military aircraft were destroyed while eight ships at anchor in the harbour were sunk. Among the casualties were hundreds of cases of burns from ships, the wharf and oil tanks at the harbour.

Sister Lorraine Blow was preparing her ward when... "There was a terrific blast which flew me off my feet into the air and down again".

The bomb blast that wounded her, killed Sister Margaret de Mestre who was preparing her ward one deck below. Sister de Mestre died from shrapnel wounds to her back and abdomen. She was 26 years old.

Sister Margaret Ewart crouched to the floor as her ward was strafed with gunfire. 'All of a sudden two fighter planes swooped down... so low we could see the pilots... that rat-a-tat-tat just above our heads ...I felt a bullet would go through me at any minute. Unfortunately, one of our patients under his bed was killed'.

Despite the destruction of hospitals and civil infrastructure, Matron Edith McQuade White prepared her nurses for hundreds of cases of burns from ships ablaze in the harbour.

She wrote in her Reminiscences of an Australian Army Nurse that: 'Every ward had wounded in every available bed, and also on the verandas".

For the next 36 hours, the Sisters worked tirelessly until 190 of the most seriously injured were transferred to the Manunda, a hospital ship that had been damaged but was still afloat in the harbour.

Loading of the wounded was the most difficult part and took hours as patients were ferried by barges from land to the Manunda anchored some distance out in the harbour. Several of the 119th AGH nurses accompanied their patients on board when she finally sailed for Perth at 11:30 pm that night.

One year later McQuade White was promoted to the rank of lieutenant colonel and appointed principal matron, Northern Territory Force, responsible for nursing services in all army hospitals in the Territory.

But not before further attacks on home soil.

The air attacks across northern Australia continued until November 1943, by which time the Japanese had raided the Top End over 200 times with bombs dropped on Townsville, Katherine, Wyndham, Derby, Port Hedland and Broome.

Contrary to widespread belief at the time, the attacks were not a precursor to an invasion. The Japanese were preparing to invade Timor, and their attacks were aimed at thwarting any counter-offensive launched from Northern Australia.

## Broome — 1942

On 3 March, nine Japanese fighter aircraft attacked the West Australian town of Broome.

During the attack, which consisted of strafing runs by the Zeros, at least 88 were killed and 24 aircraft were lost. The remote pearling port, which was virtually undefended had become a direct landing point for refugees and soldiers fleeing from the Japanese invasion just to its north. As such the human toll from the attacks was enormous.

Most of the flying boats based in Broome had been crammed with Dutch refugees when they struck. There was no escape for survivors trapped by burning fuel on the water, as well as the strong tidal currents in Roebuck Bay.

At least 40 more people are known to have died, although the exact figure, thought to be higher, may never be known.

## Sydney Submarine Attack

On or around the night of 31 May 1942, three Japanese midget submarines, each with a two-man crew, avoided a partially constructed boom net and silently slipped into Sydney Harbour. They aimed to attack allied warships.

One of the midget submarines was detected and attacked before it could cause damage. The crew of another which suffered damage scuttled their submarine and then shot themselves.

The third submarine attempted to torpedo the heavy cruiser USS Chicago but missed its target and one of the torpedoes slammed into a Garden Island Wharf retaining wall. The other drove harmlessly onto land.

The blast from the explosion destroyed 'HMAS Kuttabul' a Sydney ferry which had been converted into accommodation for naval personnel.

Twenty-one sailors were killed, nineteen of them Australian and two British.

Dozens of homes around Garden Island vibrated and shook from the impact, one witness telling The Sydney Morning Herald:

'I saw the whole ferry lift as though she were on the top of an enormous wave and then settle down again sinking at the stern ... I saw pieces of wood flying through the air. Half the steering wheel was blown away'.

According to Able Seaman Eric Davis, 'I was blown right through the roof from my bunk on the lower deck... I could not free myself for what seemed like an eternity'.

The water was up to his chest before finally being rescued.

Other survivors would describe Bandsman J Cummins as the hero of the night.

Cummins had boarded Kuttabul only five minutes before the explosion.

Despite an injured hand he immediately stripped off and dived repeatedly into the bitterly cold watery wreckage ignoring shattered glass and jagged woodwork in a frantic search for trapped survivors.

According to observers 'One of these had two broken ankles and would undoubtedly have perished but for his courage'.

Cummins is credited with rescuing three critically injured shipmates.

Ordinary Seaman LT Combers was another who disregarded his safety returned to the dangerous wreck and saved the life of another.

Australians love a hero and it seems there is even respect for the enemy.

The RAN would later recognise the bravery of the four Japanese submariners whose bodies were recovered from the two subs destroyed in Sydney Harbour. They were accorded a funeral with naval honours.

Meanwhile, the successful Japanese attacker evaded further detection and disappeared without a trace until 2006 when recreational divers discovered its wreck off Sydney's northern beaches.

## Sinking the Centaur — 1943

14 May 1943, in one of the most appalling attacks to impact mainland Australia, the Hospital Ship Centaur was attacked and sunk by a Japanese submarine off the coast of North Stradbroke Island, Queensland.

Of the 332 medical personnel and civilian crew, 268 died, including 63 of the 65 army personnel.

The attack took place at approximately 4:00 a.m. while on her second run from Sydney to Port Moresby. The torpedo struck the port side oil fuel tank creating a hole 8 to 10 metres across, igniting the fuel, and setting the ship on fire.

Many of those on board were immediately killed by concussion or perished in the inferno. The rapid sinking prevented the deployment of lifeboats, although two broke off from Centaur as she sank.

Of the 332 people on board, only 64 were rescued. Most of the crew and passengers were asleep at the time of the attack and had little chance to escape.

Although Centaur's sinking was a war crime on the hospital ship no one was ever tried for the attack and the case file was closed on 14 December 1948 without any charges laid. Historians were divided on which submarine was responsible.

Sister Ellen Savage of the Australian Army Nursing Service was the only survivor of twelve nurses.

Although suffering from severe injuries she displayed great heroism.

A strong swimmer, Savage spent two hours in the water before being dragged onto a makeshift raft. Concealing her injuries, she immediately began organising rations and raising morale among the many severely burned, until rescued 36 hours later.

Ellen Savage became only the second Australian woman to be awarded the George Medal for bravery.

According to the War Memorial Roll of Honour, 102,760 Australians have died while serving in overseas conflicts.

Australians have always celebrated their heroes and with few exceptions, they have predominantly been men serving in the military.

## Women at War

Since the beginning of 1900 when 27-year-old Ida Robertson, a young woman from Hay, New South Wales, convinced Prime Minister Edmund Barton she could help the Boer war effort, Australian women began entering war zones.

The door then opened for Matron Nellie Gould and her dedicated nurses who volunteered for Boer War service and Australian nurses have been distinguishing themselves on the front line of wars ever since.

During the South African conflict, Australia suffered its first recorded woman war casualty when nurse Frances Fanny Hines, who had served in disease-infested battle zones, died of pneumonia on 7 August 1900.

In World War 1, 2,562 Australian army nurses enlisted. 25 were killed in action.

Nancy Wake is undoubtedly Australia's most enduring war hero.

In WW2 she topped the Gestapo's most-wanted list frustrating the enemy as she led a band of the French resistance. Her fame was spread further by the Germans themselves who dubbed her 'the white mouse' because of her ability to disappear.

She is revered today as a woman of exceptional courage whose daring exploits saved hundreds of Allied lives and helped bring the Nazi occupation of France to an end.

Heroines also emerged in other theatres of war.

Vera Tornery and Margaret Anderson were recognised for their bravery after using their bodies to shield wounded passengers when the ship 'Empire Star' was bombed during the fall of Singapore.

Then on the evening of 12 February 1942, the coastal steamer 'Vyner Brooke', one of the last ships carrying evacuees from Singapore was attacked and sunk.

Among the 181 passengers were the last of 65 Australian nurses to be evacuated.

Of those nurses, 12 were killed during the air attack or drowned. A terrible fate awaited the remaining survivors.

Of those who reached Banka Island, 23 nurses were ordered into the water and machine-gunned in cold blood by the Japanese.

Sister Vivian Bullwinkle was wounded, faked her death and ultimately lived to assist others in their struggles to survive as POW's. She and colleague Agnes 'Betty' Jeffrey say we 'never lost our spirit even though we lost our strength'.

Both returned to Australia where they campaigned to raise funds for nurses killed in action. Both she and Betty Jeffrey lived until the year 2000.

Australian women served in the Boer War (1899–1902), World War I (1914–1918), World War 2 (1939–1945), The Korean War (1950–1953), The Vietnam War (1962–1972), The Gulf War (1990–1991) Iraq and Afghanistan.

And in WW2 while thousands of men were fighting overseas an army of women was serving Australia on home soil with equal acts of loyalty and incredible acts of bravery in the face of disaster.

In WW2 Australian women were also actively recruited into jobs that had previously been the preserve of men; working in factories and shipyards, as members of the Women's Land Army and actively contributing to the war effort by joining voluntary organisations to raise money to provide comforts for our troops.

While the wars in which Australia was involved inflicted profound effects on the lives of all, the many brave deeds of our women have long been overshadowed by history. And sadly, the same can also be said of our 'first nation' heroes.

## Indigenous Warriors

An unknown contingent of Aboriginal soldiers first served in the Boer War, many hiding their true heritage in order to enlist.

Up to 70 Aboriginal men served at Gallipoli, 13 of whom were killed in action.

Between 1,000 to 1,300 Indigenous soldiers served during the World War 1, of whom around 250 to 300 paid the ultimate sacrifice.

It is estimated that up to 3,000 Aboriginal or Torres Strait Islanders served in World War 2. They have since proudly participated in Korea, Vietnam, Iraq and Afghanistan and peacekeeping operations including in Somalia and East Timor.

At least 60 First Nation troops were killed in action during World War 1.

One of the fallen was Reg Rawlings awarded a medal for outstanding bravery on the Western Front. This would inspire his nephew Reg Saunders to enlist in WW2 and become the first indigenous Australian to become a commissioned officer in the armed forces. His younger brother Harry Saunders also joined the Army but was killed on the Kokoda Track in 1942.

Other Indigenous Warriors include:
- Harry Thorpe who served as an infantryman in World War I and was awarded a medal for bravery
- Marion Smith was the only Aboriginal woman known to have served in World War I.
- Frederick Prentice war hero recognised 105 years after his bravery on the Western Front.
- The Lovett brothers and their families have been recognised for their significant contribution to the Australian Military.
- Leonard 'Len' Waters Australia's first indigenous aviator served as a fighter pilot in WW2.
- Charles Mene received a medal of honour for serving in Japan and Korea.

It is hard to know the exact number of First Nation enlistees who served overseas because the Australian Defence Force did not initially record the cultural background of its members.

It is said a strong motivator for First Nation soldiers to enlist was the promise of fair treatment and equality and a promise of full citizenship rights upon their return.

However, after returning from overseas service many found cases of discrimination, colonisation and injustice were worse than when they'd left.

Despite discrimination and exclusion, thousands of Aboriginal and Torres Strait Islander peoples have served in the Australian Defence Forces since the 1860s and possibly earlier.

Today they continue to serve Australia wherever and whenever they are needed.

Defending our coastline is NORFORCE the largest army surveillance unit in the world, which has over sixty per cent Aboriginal and Torres Strait Islander personnel.

Its history goes back to the 'Nackeroos' — a Northern Territory Special Reconnaissance Unit and Twenty-First Observer Unit formed during World War 2 as a coastal patrol amid fears of a Japanese invasion.

\* \* \* \*

At dawn on 25 April 1915, Australian troops took part in the Allied invasion of Turkey's Gallipoli Peninsula. The popular notion is that the failed campaign forged the most fundamental turning point in the creation of Australia's identity.

However, World War 2 was just as significant in the fight for a national identity.

In response to the bombing of Darwin in 1942 and subsequent attacks on Australian soil, the government recalled its forces from the Middle East.

Later that year the Government declared to the world Australia had become a 'sovereign nation'.

There is no time more than in war when ideals and heroes are born, regardless of race or gender. Lest we forget.

However, lest not forget our other heroes. Those who helped forge the identity of a nation and helped define who we are as a people. Each of us may have worshipped a hero from time to time, whether they represented politics, sport, the indigenous, science or even entertainment.

It is a very subjective list but researching history several names continually emerge after having left their lasting legacy.

(With acknowledgement to the Australian War Memorial)

# Heroes of the Past

**In no particular order.**

1. Andrew 'Banjo' Paterson, the bush poet who left an intrinsic legacy.

2. Sir Donald Bradman, the world's most dominant sportsman.

3. Sir Howard Florey helped save millions through Penicillin.

4. Mary MacKillop — Australia's Saint.

5. Eddie Mabo changed a law and raised the spiritual bond between indigenous people and the land.

6. Sir John Monash was a man born to lead.

7. Sir Douglas Mawson was a scientist and courageous solo adventurer.

8. Edith Cowan — prominent in the women's suffrage movement.

9. Albert Jacka, whose heroics made him a Gallipoli legend.

10. Sir Edward 'Weary' Dunlop — a revered figure in history.

11. Nancy Wake "The White Mouse" the most wanted WW2 spy in France.

12. Sir Charles Kingsford Smith pioneer of long-distance flight.

13. Phar Lap, "Big Red" the horse that helped a nation through depression.

14. Lawrence Hargrave the father of flight.

15. Dame Nellie Melba the greatest soprano of her era.

16. Caroline Chisholm found lodgings and jobs for more than 10,000 women.

17. Sir Henry Parkes the Father of Federation.

18. Rupert Murdoch became a global media colossus.

19. Slim Dusty — National Treasure.

20. Unsung Heroes *

* Unsung heroes vastly outnumber awarded heroes. They are everyday people who achieve extraordinary things by selflessly caring for others.

From healthcare workers and first responders during times of pandemics to community volunteers who risk their own lives during times of floods, fires and personal crises. Many heroes are born out of disasters but unsung heroes are those who step up voluntarily often putting their own lives on the line in the process.

'Unsung heroes' is perhaps a cliché, but it demonstrates an extraordinary spirit that has proudly become part of the Australian psyche.

My Country — Dorothea Mackellar
*The love of field and coppice*
*Of green and shaded lanes,*
*Of ordered woods and gardens*
*Is running in your veins.*
*Strong love of grey-blue distance,*
*Brown streams and soft, dim skies*
*I know, but cannot share it,*
*My love is otherwise.*
*I love a sunburnt country,*
*A land of sweeping plains,*
*Of ragged mountain ranges,*
*Of droughts and flooding rains.*
*I love her far horizons,*
*I love her jewel sea,*
*Her beauty and her terror*
*The wide brown land for me!*
*The stark white ring-barked forests,*
*All tragic to the moon,*
*The sapphire-misted mountains,*
*The hot gold hush of noon,*
*Green tangle of the brushes*
*Where lithe lianas coil,*
*And orchids deck the tree tops,*

*And ferns the warm dark soil.*
*Core of my heart, my country!*
*Her pitiless blue sky,*
*When, sick at heart, around us*
*We see the cattle die*
*But then the grey clouds gather,*
*And we can bless again*
*The drumming of an army,*
*The steady soaking rain.*
*Core of my heart, my country!*
*Land of the rainbow gold,*
*For flood and fire and famine*
*She pays us back threefold.*
*Over the thirsty paddocks,*
*Watch, after many days,*
*The filmy veil of greenness*
*That thickens as we gaze.*

## BE PUBLISHED

Publish through a successful publisher.
Brolga Publishing is represented through:
• National book trade distribution, including sales, marketing & distribution through Simon & Schuster.
• International book trade distribution to:
    - The United Kingdom
    - Sales representation in South East Asia
• Worldwide e-Book distribution

For details and enquiries, contact: Brolga Publishing Pty Ltd
ABN 46 063 962 443
PO Box 452
Torquay Victoria 3228
Australia

markzocchi@brolgapublishing.com.au
(Email for a catalogue request)